CARING ENOUGH TO
CONFRONT

A sequel to
Five Seconds at a Time: How Leaders
Can Make the Impossible Possible

Dr. Denis S. J. Shackel

Tellwell Talent
www.tellwell.ca

ISBN
978-0-2288-2563-0 (Hardcover)
978-0-2288-2562-3 (Paperback)
978-0-2288-2564-7 (eBook)

"As a specialist in human resource development, Denis Shackel presents workshops designed to unlock the talents of those within leadership and management in business and government organizations."

Clients include J. D. Irving Ltd., Accenture, IBM, Royal Bank of Canada, Burger King, Bayer, RCMP, Chrysler, Maple Leaf Foods and Bell Canada.

"With an underlying theme of love and respect, Dr. Shackel shares his extensive knowledge and personal experience to supply the reader with a wealth of information to successfully handle difficult conversations. This book needs to be on every leader's shelf!"

Judy Steeper

"Simply put, I am the person I am today because of the influence of Dr. Denis Shackel. As my professor, mentor and friend, he's shown me my potential and inspired me to lean into it for the benefit of those I serve. In this book, he's unpacked a crucial skill and attribute all truly human leaders hone – having the conversations that help people grow stronger together. The use of story, thought provoking questions and actionable steps bring the message to life. I've never heard of a relationship or organizational culture that improves with less communication. Dr. Shackel provides an inspiring, clear, practical and proven method to use care and communication as the tools to help you and your people achieve the seemingly impossible."

Stephen Shedletzky
Former Student Executive Coach, Purpose Whisper,
Father and Leadership & Culture Development Specialist

"An extremely timely and crucial book for any business leader. An exceptional sequel to Denis's first text book, dealing with an increasingly important topic, amplified by the fallout from COVID-19."

Michael Sider, PhD
Head of Management Communication
Ivey School of Business Western University, Canada

Dr. Shackel's new work provides fresh insights into ideas previously put forward by others. His insistence on empathy as a key component in conducting difficult conversations offers a novel approach. The reader will discover the necessary steps to be taken in conducting difficult conversations that will lead to successful conclusions.

W. Stirling Kenny J.D.

ACKNOWLEDGEMENTS

- Alyza Nykhol Alenton
- Mary Lynn Fluter-Shackel
- Kathleen and Bruce Macgregor
- Alison Strumberger, Jun Mark Vertudazo, and Simon Ogden

In *Caring Enough to Confront,* Denis uses a blend of academic research and personal stories to forge a personal connection with the reader, exhibiting the teachings required to have challenging conversations. This approach is a masterful extension of Denis's in-person lessons, where he coaches people to lean into difficult situations, embrace failure, and self-correct in order to grow as leaders.

Scott Loveland
MBA, Ivey Business School
B.E.Sc. Biochemical Engineering

TABLE OF CONTENTS

SECTION A: ATTITUDE

SECTION B: BEHAVIOUR

SECTION C: C. A. R. I. N. G.

FOREWORD

I met Denis 24 years ago when I was CEO of Webplan (now called Kinaxis). I had just become CEO of the company, which was failing and out of money. I made the difficult decision to take the company into bankruptcy which meant laying off my leadership team and 2/3rds of the employees and closing the field offices. We were days away from shutting the doors if we did not get protection from the bankruptcy courts. I also needed to secure venture funding to try to save the company and move forward. I had been in leadership positions previously, but this was the first time for me to be in the lead role where the stakes were so high. I needed help.

Three years into the turnaround, I invited Denis to train our newly formed executive team on leadership and communication skills that could strengthen us as a team as we focused on executing our new business strategy. That 5-day course became the foundation for our company's future success and little did I know at the time, the foundation for my coaching practice developing the leadership skills of senior level executives.

Since that training program, I have either led companies or been the executive coach to hundreds of top business leaders around the world. Kinaxis has grown from $2 million in annual revenue during the turnaround to become a publicly traded company with a $5.28 billion market value. I truly believe Denis's training and continued guidance were instrumental to our learning and mastering the skills necessary to be a world class company, a highly effective team and compassionate leaders.

In this book, Denis's second, he offers real life scenarios that not only demonstrate effective leadership lessons but extends those examples as a blueprint for living a more authentic life. To me, living a more authentic life means communicating honestly and compassionately with others. That is not always easy. The mere idea of being completely honest with someone can be so daunting and fearful that many people will avoid the hard conversations to share their truth. As a result, they will live a life that can be filled with pain, regret, resentment, or anger. Not the qualities we think of when we think of authentic.

What is the hardest conversation you have ever had to have with someone? Do you remember the angst, the anxiety, and the adrenaline that rushed through your body in preparation for having that conversation? Were you scared by the thought of how the other person would react? Did you postpone the conversation for the "right time", only to have time lapse for so long to make a difference or think it is too late to change now? We are not taught as children or adults how to have a difficult conversation. We are taught to communicate on so many other levels but not about the most challenging subjects of all. We are so ill prepared to confront the elephant in the room or to share the feelings that we have held inside for so long.

The first day of the training class, Denis came into the conference room with 10 leaders from our executive team and told us the story of losing his brother-in-law Bruce on the mountaintop and the incredible night he spent trying to stay alive until the next morning. Denis was crying as he shared this harrowing story with us. We did not realize at the time what an incredible gift he had just given us. He showed us true leadership is vulnerable. He was open, raw, and emotional. He gave us all permission to be vulnerable during that 5-day meeting. It was the most productive meeting we had ever had and set the stage for how we would communicate for the years to come. Denis shared during the training that "leaders must show vulnerability first" so that their team sees that it is safe to be open. He taught us this leadership lesson by demonstrating it at the beginning of our training. Yes, he was crying in front of a team of strangers in the first 15 minutes of meeting him but that is what made the program so compelling and truly authentic. I still share that story today with my executive coaching clients as an amazing example of how leaders need to be able to create a safe place for their people and encourage them to be vulnerable. This shows strength not weakness. This same lesson holds true outside a company. It is true for families, for spouses, for any relationship dynamic where ideas or opinions will not always be aligned and agreed upon. Disagreements, arguments, and conflict are bound to happen from time to time and when it does, how do you address it? Does the situation grow so big and untenable that it becomes a challenging conversation? And if so, do you confront it?

Denis describes in *Caring Enough to Confront*, the results of his survey of 7,082 executives where 49% of the respondents avoided challenging conversations at all costs. 48% made the effort to confront, although not successfully and only 3% felt they were successful in confronting the challenging conversation. How is it possible that 49% of executives avoided challenging conversations, and the confrontation that comes with it at all costs? In what productive and thriving organization is avoidance, at that level, acceptable? It is not a deliberate, conscious choice on the part of these leaders but rather the slow and steady building of the day-to-day pressures that postpone the "hard conversations" until another day. Combine procrastination with a lack of communications training and you have the underpinnings for a challenged confrontation.

The behavioral personality theory known as DiSC® profiling was not a subject taught in my college business classes, nor had I learned how to apply Maslow's Hierarchy of Needs in a professional setting. I had not heard of Neuro Linguistic Programming or NLP, until Denis Shackel walked through our doors at Webplan (now Kinaxis). The skills to identify different personality traits and then to flex to the very different behavioral styles than our own to communicate more effectively, was a game changer for us. Just as Denis brought those new concepts to us then, he brings a new perspective to us now within these pages.

Denis's insight, wisdom and experience come from a long career of helping thousands of executives to become better leaders by becoming better communicators. He explains that all tough relationships, conflicts, and communication breakdowns such as disagreements, divorce, family estrangement and even war, are all due to our inability to deal with our differences.

It should be as no surprise to those who know Denis, that this is where he asserts that Love, Forgiveness and Fear are the catalysts for reconciliation and understanding. Leadership, as he explains, is a thought choice. Good leaders deliberately choose to accept that the truth can be painful and uncomfortable. A weak leader will edit the truth and choose not to face it. To have a successful challenging conversation, one needs to start with Love. We need to see the other person with love, compassion, and understanding the issue through their eyes. If this person has wronged us, Denis reminds us, that forgiveness is the highest form of love and the highest form of understanding.

Fear, Denis explains is the basis for us avoiding a difficult conversation. He provides many examples that if we can reject fear and move into these difficult conversations with love, we can be successful. This is what Denis means when someone *Cares Enough to Confront*.

An interesting aside is that in one of our recent conversations, Denis shared with me the fact that he was contemplating changing the book title to *May I Be Brutally Honest?* The word brutally would have a large red X slashed through it. His argument was that while to be brutally honest is a common and frequently used expression, the X would stress his conviction that there is no place for brutality in any relationship …. Professional or personal. He obviously chose to keep the original title, but has nonetheless conveyed throughout the book the importance of avoiding brutality at all costs. Caring (loving) conquers all.

Denis taught us years ago about compassionate leadership and communications, but it seems even more important and relevant today. They say leadership shows up in the tough times more than the easy times. After all, most leaders can look good when their product, market or economy is doing well. In our post COVID reality, where relationship dynamics and challenging conversations are at their most strained levels in years, we need a playbook to guide us through our new normal.

Caring Enough to Confront is that playbook. It shows us how to lead, confront and communicate from a position of love, understanding and compassion.

Michael Ker
Executive Coach
Olympic Swimmer 1976
Former CEO of Webplan, now Kinaxis

Chapter 1

My Most Challenging Conversation

Meeting Kathleen

There she was. The tarmac was spinning in front of me.

I saw her as soon as I was helped out of the rescue helicopter. She was standing, waiting, sobbing.

My beloved sister Kathleen appeared to be propped up by two women, whom I later learned were volunteer bereavement counsellors. I could not manage to walk, so she broke from the women and ran toward me. We grasped each other and sobbed uncontrollably in locked embrace. For a long time neither of us seemed able to speak; we allowed our bodies to tremor in each other's grasp until our breathing seemed miraculously to get in sync.

One of the most difficult conversations of my life, which became a defining moment for me, began by Kathleen saying, "Thank goodness it wasn't you."

Those words haunted me for the next three years, before I eventually plucked up the courage to ask Kathleen what she had meant by them. This was the morning after the longest night of my life, a night in which, but by the grace of God, I should have perished. The day before, my beloved brother-in-law Bruce, Kathleen's husband, was my leader and guide as we climbed Mount Ruapehu in New Zealand on May 17, 1997.

At approximately 8,000 feet, Bruce slipped as a result of his crampons breaking, slid down the sheer rock face we were climbing, and disappeared from view. At the time, I did not know he had almost instantly died. I was stranded near the top of the mountain and had to spend the night in minus-30-degree temperatures dressed only in a sunhat, T-shirt, shorts, and boots.

Details of how I managed to survive the eight hours before I was rescued by helicopter the next morning are presented in the book *Five Seconds at a Time: How leaders make the impossible possible*,[1] the forerunner to this text. More significantly, however, it documents how in the very last split second, Bruce had chosen to pull his hand back from grasping my out-stretched hand to catch him as he plunged by me.

His choice remains the most treasured second I have experienced in my life, and up to now I have been alive for well over 2,920,000,000 seconds. I am absolutely certain that I would not have lived to chronicle his story had he taken my hand. The profound choice he made in that split second surely illustrates that "greater love hath no man than he lay down his life for his friend."[2]

Bruce died that I might live.

This then, was the context within which I was now called to have a terrifying conversation with my sister. My fears were fuel to a flood of questions.

Would she even want to talk with me?

Would she be furious with me because it was my idea to climb the mountain?

Would she think it my fault Bruce was dead?

Would she really believe that it was Bruce and not me that pulled his hand back?

Would I be able to explain what happened?

Would she reject me and end our relationship?

This moment with Kathleen forever changed how I approach difficult, even scary interactions, and this became part of my life's work. In hindsight, I can also identify additional key questions which arise when we are faced with potentially challenging conversations.

Shall I simply avoid the issue and hope it fades away?

Will I take my responsibility as a key player in the issue?

Am I prepared to listen?

Will I seek first to understand before being understood?

Is the relationship important enough to me to justify going through the time, effort, and probable pain of coming to closure?

Is my motive self-serving or fuelled by compassion?

Am I sufficiently self-disciplined to be able to manage my anger?

Am I operating out of spite, resentment or fury?

Can I forgive?

What part is my own ego playing in this confrontation?

Am I in a state of self-doubt, embarrassment, shame, procrastination, insecurity?

Do I *really* care enough to confront?

Personal background note

The tragic death of my brother-in-law Bruce while we were climbing Mount Ruapehu became the stimulus to the writing of this book. The life-changing experience of spending an eight-hour night at minus-30 degrees C while wearing only a sunhat, T-shirt, shorts, socks, and boots left me with bone-marrow-deep leadership lessons. These lessons, which have continued to inspire my teaching and consulting over the last twenty years, include the following:

The profound significance of thought choice

In our moments of decision our destiny is determined.[3]

Decisions are ultimately a consequence of our *thought choice.* Nobody chooses thoughts for us. We must take responsibility and be accountable for the thought choices we make.

I now define leadership as a thought choice rather than a title, a *disposition* rather than a *position.*

On Mount Ruapehu I chose to think, envision, and ultimately believe that I would see the rising sun. This vision not only saved my life but was, in its initial stages, a thought which grew to an emotionally charged vision, and finally an expectation. The fact that the expectation became a reality is why I'm alive today, and why I passionately see leadership as beginning with a person becoming a leader only when they think of and see themselves as one. It is well documented[4,5,6] that we become what we think. It becomes imperative that leaders think, see, and feel themselves as leaders if they are to fulfill their desire or goal to become one. The initial step in this sequence is thought choice.

Equally significant is the fact that our perception is selective. It is impossible for us to be simultaneously aware of the thousands of stimuli which are bombarding us internally as well as externally. Writers such as John Assaraf[7] and Steven Aitchison[8] claim we are bombarded by 75 gigabytes of information and 30–40,000 thoughts of our own each day. Therefore, we are selective in the ones we choose to perceive with our conscious mind.

This selectivity is also a consequence of our thought choice. As Paul Simon beautifully words it in his lyrics to the song "The Boxer," *Man hears what he wants to hear and disregards the rest.*

It's all thought choice, nonetheless.

The necessity to develop an initial thought choice into a vivid vision

I am absolutely certain that the vision of seeing the rising sun literally saved my life. I now have a bone-marrow depth of conviction that King Solomon was correct when he claimed that "Where there is no vision, people perish."[9]

The profound value of what I now like to call the "Five-Second Principle"

This involves the following series of steps:

1. Breathe and pause to reflect on the goal. This involves stepping back before stepping forward (reflectively tell the truth).
2. Prioritize what is of the greatest importance.
3. Break the seemingly insurmountable challenges into smaller, more manageable ones.
4. Identify the first step.
5. Take the first "bite" to eat the "elephant."

An equally passionate belief which has guided my personal as well as professional life since the mountaintop experience is the fundamental importance of what the Japanese have coined as *kaizen*, or "constant improvement."

What's the point of life if we cannot learn from our experiences and contribute to make a positive difference in the lives of those with whom we are privileged to live and work? I have therefore adopted a practice, a habit, of closing each day with the question: "If I had today again, what would I do differently?" I do this in the name of attempting to learn from the experiences of the past day in order to live a more fruitful day the next.

The lessons learned while facing death at high altitudes, combined with the habit of constant improvement—*kaizen*—have prompted me to turn my gaze from the 8,000 feet of Mount Ruapehu to the 29,029 feet of Mount Everest, and lift my horizons to even greater heights.

Perhaps I have also been influenced by the fact that Sir Edmund Hillary (a fellow New Zealander, and a hero of mine) practised on Mount Cook, the highest mountain in New Zealand, before making history on May 29, 1953, when he and Sherpa Tenzing Norgay became the first to stand on top of Mount Everest, the "roof of the world."

Ironically, Bruce persuaded me not to climb Mount Cook because many had lost their lives there. He convinced me that it would be more responsible to climb "easy, safe Ruapehu." How ironic!

Scope of the book

What are the best practices to handle challenging conversations successfully?

Napoleon defined a leader as a "dealer in hope." This book deals in that hope and goes beyond what other writers have suggested as solutions to difficult conversations.

Caring is the key word.

Caring as dramatically and inimitably portrayed by Bruce pulling his hand back. A profound selflessness.

Caring as shown by Kathleen, who, after tragically losing Bruce, climbed Mount Ruapehu. Her motive was not just to overcome the fear and deal with the pain associated with the mountain, but to stock the hut with supplies of tinned food, blankets, and water bottles, on the off-chance that someone else would find themselves in the precarious position her brother did.

Caring to remember that, as Theodore Roosevelt said, "Nobody cares how much you know, until they know how much you care."[10]

Caring to go beyond five seconds at a time. Yes, I am adamant about the profound value of the Five Seconds at a Time principle presented above, but while I believe it to be necessary, I no longer believe it is sufficient.

Since writing the last book, I have been struck with the inadequacy of five seconds—it's far too long a period to deal with the foundational importance of thought choice over what can commonly present itself as more like *one* second or less.

To be successful with challenging conversations we must monitor and choose constructive thoughts every second. The title of the book could well be *Challenging Conversations, Moment by Moment.*

Caring to commit.

> *Until one cares to commit, there is hesitancy, the chance to draw back, always ineffectiveness. Concerning all acts of initiative and creation, there is one elementary truth, the ignorance of which kills countless ideas and splendid plans: that the moment one definitely commits oneself, then Providence moves too.*
>
> – W.H. Murray, the Scottish Himalayan Expedition, 1951[11]

Caring unconditionally.

Easy words to say, but necessary to implement in order to move beyond previously published models for dealing with difficult conversations.

This book explores why challenging conversations are difficult, why we avoid them, and why we often handle them poorly. While it is written primarily for leaders, the text addresses a critical aspect of human interaction and thus applies to how we deal with our children, parents, partners, ex-wives or husbands, colleagues, friends, and neighbours.

Procedural steps are outlined on how to experience great fulfillment in any relationship, whether personal or professional.

These steps and skills can

- transform a serious disagreement between business partners from a political power struggle into a powerhouse for innovation and breakthrough.
- rekindle loving relationships within a marriage.
- turn a war zone between management and unions, or between parents and teenagers, or between siblings within a family, into a harmonizing zone of trust, safety, and genuine caring.
- facilitate healing within businesses, between colleagues and team members, and amongst neighbours.

These are the skills to acknowledge the elephant in the room and, step by step, successfully deal with the obvious and stinking carcass. It is argued herein that

- the life-saving lessons learned facing death at 8,000 feet during the longest night of my life have equally profound lessons for daylight hours.
- successful people rise to the top when they choose mental sets which ensure productive, satisfying resolutions at the close of challenging conversations.

Introductory definitions

> *Any time we feel vulnerable or our self-esteem is implicated, when the issues at stake are important and the outcome is uncertain, when we care deeply about what is being discussed or about the people with whom we are discussing it, there is a potential for us to experience the conversation as difficult.*
>
> – Douglas Stone, et al., from *Difficult Conversations*[12]

A challenging conversation is anything you find difficult to talk about, such as

- ending a relationship (personal or professional).
- asking for a raise.
- presenting a critical performance review.
- saying no to someone in need.
- confronting abusive or disrespectful behaviour.
- saying sorry.
- disagreeing with the majority.

These are all challenging conversations, which are characterized by the following common elements:

- Differing opinions
- Emotionally charged situations
- High stakes

Whether to avoid or confront—why is that key question so difficult? Probably because *we already know the truth*.

If we avoid it, feelings will fester. If we confront it we may be rejected, and the relationship might deteriorate. Equally truthful is the conclusion that there is no diplomatic way for a leader to fire his or her friend. "There is no such thing as a diplomatic hand grenade," writes Doug Stone in *Difficult Conversations*.[13] Coated with sugar, thrown hard or softly, a hand grenade is going to damage.

Tact is not the simple answer. There is no way to deliver a difficult message with tact or outrun the consequences. Furthermore, choosing *not* to deliver the message is equivalent to hanging on to the hand grenade once you have pulled the pin. A challenging conversation avoided is a challenging conversation multiplied!

Besides, the future is scary, particularly when we try to avoid it.

Perhaps most importantly of all, trust (surely the ultimate intangible in any relationship, personal or professional) is built on telling the truth, not on telling people what they necessarily want to hear.

Critical importance of this topic

In his ground-breaking book *Guns, Germs, and Steel*,[14] evolutionary biologist Jared Diamond stunningly dismantles radically based theories of human history by revealing the environmental factors actually responsible for history's broadest patterns. It is a history of the world's peoples, a unified narrative of human life even more intriguing and important than accounts of dinosaurs and glaciers.

Beginning 13,000 years ago, when the Stone Age hunter-gatherers constituted the entire human population, paths of development of human societies on different continents began to diverge greatly. Early domestication of wild plants and animals in the Fertile Crescent (Turkey), China and Mesoamerica gave the peoples of those regions a head start in developing more complex societies. But the unequal rates at which food production spread from these regions had much to do with the nature and social developments within these societies.

Peoples who could create harmonious communities—and obviously deal successfully with disagreements—were more likely to develop writing, technology, government, and organized religions, as well as potent weapons of war. It was those societies, adventuring on sea and land, that expanded the homelands at the expense of other peoples.

> Societies that adopt new crops, livestock or technology do so *only if social interactions and communications between their peoples was successful to enable them to nourish themselves better and to outbreed, displace, conquer or kill off societies resisting them.* Any two villagers getting into an argument will share kin, who predictably apply pressure on

them to deal successfully with difficult conversations and keep them from becoming violent.

– From *Guns, Germs, and Steel* (emphasis mine)[15]

An equally respected writer on the history and evolution of man is Edward Gibbon, who wrote *The History of the Decline and Fall of the Roman Empire* in 1776. Within the introduction of a 2005 edition of this monumental work, Daniel Boorstin states:

> Few books have been so widely and indiscriminately praised and recognized as authoritative. Gibbons is one of the few writers who hold as high a place in the history of literature.[16]

Gibbons draws our attention to the critical importance of the challenging conversations when he states:

> Differences in opinion and potential *difficult conversations* [emphasis mine] between Emperors invariably were avoided. Resorting to order any hesitation of opposition was the beginning of the fall of civilization.

Of all new passions and appetites, the love of power is the most impervious and miserable nature, since the pride of one man requires the submission of the multitude.

After the extinction of paganism, the Christians in peace and love might have enjoyed their solitary triumph. But the principle of discord was alive in their bosom, and became one of the challenges inherent within serious conversations/human intention, they were more solicitous to explore the nature than to practice the laws of their founder.[17]

Further evidence of the crucial importance of the topic of challenging conversations is powerfully presented by research[18] that indicates half of the world will tend to choose #1 from the following three options:

1. Avoid challenging conversations.
2. Face challenging conversations and manage them poorly.
3. Face challenging conversations and manage them effectively.

These staggering data do nothing other than stress the alarming need to address this critical topic.

Yet another key reason justifies the close study and mastery of this topic. It is widely acknowledged that how we handle challenging conversations determines the quality of relationship we have with another person. As Stone et al. state:

> What we learn is that crucial conversations transform people and relationships. They create an entirely new level of bonding. They create what Buddhism calls the "middle way" . . . not a compromise between two opposites on a straight-line continuum, but a higher middle way, like the apex of a triangle.[19]

The popular text entitled *Crucial Conversations: Tools for Talking When Stakes Are High* by Kerry Patterson et al. sums up the importance for leaders by reporting that:

> Twenty-five years of research with 20,000 people and hundreds of organizations has taught us that individual leaders who are most influential, are those who master their crucial conversations.[20]

Furthermore, McCall, Lombardo and Morrison[21] recently reported data which indicates the value and respect that 290 executives from six major corporations gave to the learning and career benefits attributed to the following five different categories:

- Course work: 9 percent
- Hardships: 19 percent
- Coaches/mentors: 21 percent
- Challenging conversations: 38 percent
- Miscellaneous: 13 percent

Personal note

These data initially surprised me when I discovered them. However, the more I have reflected upon the implications, the more I have become prepared to recognize that what leadership success I have accomplished can be attributed to learnings in the following proportions:

Figure 1: Personal Illustrations of McCall's Research with Executives

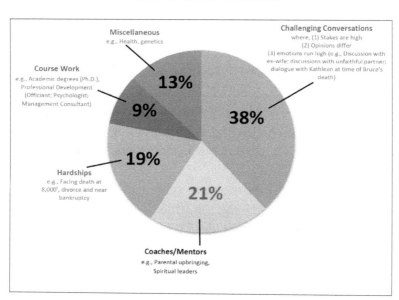

I trust that my personal example illustrates how this book is equally relevant to personal relationships, including the most intimate. Marriage counsellors will generally agree with the way Everett Worthington, in his classic text *Hope-Focused Marriage Counselling*,[22] stated the determining influence of a couple's ability to handle challenging conversations: "Readiness to deal with challenging conversations largely determines whether a couple will stay married or separate."

We further disillusion ourselves by holding up the family as a priority in our lives. The data do not support our truthfulness: 51 percent of murders and assaults are within families,[23] 36 percent of rapes are among families, and 81 percent of assailants are known to the victim.[24]

Summary

A horrific tragedy made me come face to face with the most challenging conversation of my life, leading me to begin work on this text.

Chapter 1 defines the concept of *thought choice*, and provides an overview of the Five-Second Principle presented in my previous volume, *Five Seconds at a Time*. The idea of *kaizen*—"constant improvement"—is introduced and will be discussed in detail in Chapter 7. The book's key word is introduced, *caring*, and the definition of challenging conversation is discussed, as is why mastering it is crucial to our healthy work life and personal well-being.

Chapter 1 also uses the true account of the author caring enough to confront his sister Kathleen with the reality that her husband Bruce was now dead as a result of persuading his brother-in-law to climb Mt. Ruapehu with him. The fear in approaching this challenging conversation was particularly vivid, as it was predicted to involve differences of opinion. The stakes were high, and the scenario was charged with high emotion. This true story is used throughout the book as an extreme example of the kind of challenging conversation men and women around the world experience in both their work and personal lives.

This first chapter presents the scope of the book and the critical importance of the topic, which research findings show determines the quality of the relationships we have with others.

Points to Ponder

1. What for you is a true example of a challenging conversation you know in your heart you need to address?
2. Record at least one challenging conversation from your personal life, and at least one from your work world.
3. Identify specific reasons for avoiding them. What are the outcomes if you avoid confronting the other(s)? What are the probable outcomes if you do confront them?
4. Challenging conversations delayed, become challenging conversations multiplied.

Chapter 2

Current Research on Challenging Conversations

How do people generally handle challenging conversations? Authorities such as those within the Harvard Negotiation Project[25] conclude that the answer is simple: poorly, if at all. Discussing what matters most is surprisingly difficult for people.

> *In both negotiations and daily life, for good reasons or bad, we often don't talk to each other, and don't want to. And sometimes when we do talk, things only get worse. Feelings—anger, guilt, hurt—escalate. We become more and more sure that we are right, and so do those with whom we disagree.*[26]
>
> – From *Crucial Conversations: Tools for Talking When Stakes are High*[27]

The most frequently recognized authorities and their well-regarded books in the field of challenging conversations are

- **Douglas Stone, Bruce Patton, and Sheila Heen:** *Difficult Conversations: How to Discuss What Matters Most.*[28]
- **Kerry Patterson, Joseph Grenny, Ron McMillan, and Al Switzler:** *Crucial Conversations: Tools for Talking When Stakes are High,*[29] and *Crucial Confrontations: Tools for*

Resolving Broken Promises, Violated Expectations and Bad Behaviour.[30]

- **Richard S. Gallagher:** *How to Tell Anyone Anything: Breakthrough Techniques for Handling Difficult Conversations at Work.*[31]

These titles all suggest practical tools, techniques, methodologies, and strategies for dealing with challenging conversations.

Looking at these three schools of thought in more detail will help the reader understand the complexities of challenging conversations more fully.

Stone, Patton, and Heen have compiled what is commonly known as the Harvard Negotiation Project, wherein they argue that there are in fact three conversations within any difficult conversation.

1. **The "What Happened?" conversation:** Challenging conversations involve disagreement about what has happened or should have happened. Who said what, and who did what? Who's right, who meant what, and who's to blame?

2. **The feelings conversation:** Every challenging conversation asks and answers questions about feelings. Are my feelings valid? Are they appropriate? Should I acknowledge or deny them, put them on the table, or check them at the door? What do I do about the other person's feelings? What if they are angry or hurt?

3. **The Identity Conversation:** This is the conversation we each have with ourselves about what this situation means to us. We conduct an internal debate over whether this means we're competent or incompetent, a good person or bad, worthy of love or unlovable. What impact might it have on our self-esteem and self-image, our future, and our well-being?

Our answers to these questions determine how balanced we feel during the conversations, or whether we feel off-centred and anxious.

Patterson, Grenny, McMillan, and Switzler argue in their texts that defining moments in our lives and careers normally involve "breakthrough conversations" with important people in emotionally charged situations, where decisions made take us down one of several paths.

Their work seems based on the observation made by the British historian Arnold Toynbee, who said that you can pretty well summarize all of history in this one sentence: "Nothing fails like success when you rely on it too much."[32] In other words, when a challenge in life is met by a response that is equal to it, you have success. But when the challenge moves to a higher level, the old once-successful response no longer works, and it fails. Thus, nothing fails like success.

Just as the world is changing at frightening speed and we become increasingly and profoundly interdependent, through marvellous and potentially dangerous technologies, so too have the stresses and pressures we all experience exponentially increased. This charged atmosphere makes it all the more imperative that we nourish our relationships and develop tools and an enhanced capacity to find new and better solutions to our problems.

These solutions will not interrupt *my* way or *your* way, they will need to represent *our* way. The solutions must be synergistic. Such synergy may manifest itself in a better decision and/or better relationship. Successfully handling crucial conversations therefore is an enormously important step toward a better life.

Patterson et al. make what they acknowledge as "an audacious claim": "Master your crucial conversations and you'll kick-start your career, strengthen your relationships and improve your health. As you and others master your high-stakes discussions you'll also revitalize your organization and your community."

They also report that with twenty thousand people and hundreds of organizations, the individuals who are the most influential, the ones who get things done and at the same time build relationships, are the ones who master their crucial conversations. The text gives proof that you don't have to choose between being honest and effective. You don't have to choose between candour and career. They give examples of people who routinely hold crucial conversations and hold them well, people who are able to express controversial and even risky opinions in a way that gets heard.

Furthermore, they found that successfully dealing with crucial conversations determined organizational performance. They began their twenty-five-year study assuming that a company's bottom line would depend primarily upon their performance in management systems and/or company structure, strategy, and information systems. They report being wrong! Five hundred exceptionally productive organizations revealed that peak performance had absolutely nothing to do with forms, procedures, and policies that drive performance management. In fact, over half of the highflyers had almost no performance management processes.

It all came down to how they handled crucial conversations within high-performing companies with employees who failed to deliver on their promises.

The remainder of their texts present some practical techniques for dealing with challenging conversations successfully.

- Increase your self-awareness by noticing when safety is at risk.
- Once you spot safety risks in a conversation, step out of the conversation, build and restore safety, then step back in and dialogue as best you can.
- Stay in the dialogue even when you are angry, hurt, or scared by telling stories.
- Explore other's viewpoints by the following sequence:

o **Ask:** Start by simply expressing interest in the other person's views.

o **Mirror:** Increase safety by respectfully acknowledging the emotions people appear to be feeling.

o **Paraphrase:** As others begin to share their story, restate what you've heard to show not just that you understand, but also that it's safe for them to share what they're thinking.

o **Prime:** If others continue to hold back, *prime* them by taking your best guess at what they may be thinking and feeling.

As you begin to share your views, remember the ABCs of effective communication:

- **Agree:** Agree out loud when you do.
- **Build:** If others leave something out, agree where you do, then build on what they have established.
- **Compare:** When you do differ significantly, don't suggest others are wrong. Compare your two views.

Gallagher, in his text *How to Tell Anyone Anything,*[33] presents techniques for handling difficult conversations at work. He argues that we must in all circumstances adopt a candid approach. Simply tell the truth and adopt the following three techniques:

1. Open the conversation with the "I technique": relate things to your own perspective and your own behaviour or observations, particularly when someone has made a mistake.
2. Ask questions as opposed to making statements.
3. Normalize the situation by (1) acknowledging that you recognize the other's feelings, (2) validating the other's

feelings, (3) identifying yourself as having experienced the other's feelings, and (4) incentivizing the outcome by focusing the discussion on the strongest possible benefits to the other person.

Data collected for this study

Having gained approval from the ethics committee at Western University in London, Ontario, I surveyed leaders within

- the alumni of Ivey Business School at Western,
- LinkedIn and Facebook,
- MBA and HBA classes through Ivey, and
- participants in executive development courses presented through Ivey.

By using surveymonkey.com, the data remained anonymous and totalled a sample of 7,082 people ranging from 20 to 65 years of age. The survey instrument is presented below.

Challenging Conversations Survey

Dear Participant,

I would be most grateful if you would kindly reflect on your experiences over the years you have been in leadership positions, both professional and personal.

How frequently have you dealt with challenging conversations? For purposes of my research sponsored by our school, I am defining a challenging conversation as one where (1) the stakes are high, (2) emotions are high, (3) opinions differ significantly.

These data will remain anonymous and I fervently request that you share your frequency percentages honestly and accurately.

1. % of challenging conversations I have avoided = _____

2. % of challenging conversations I have confronted and failed to resolve = _____

3. % of challenging conversations I have confronted and resolved successfully = _____

Deeply appreciated,
Dr. Denis Shackel
Professor, Management Communications
Ivey Business School

dshackel@ivey.ca

The dramatic findings showed the somewhat alarming fact that

- 49 percent of subjects "avoided at all costs,"
- 48 percent of subjects confronted unsuccessfully, and
- 3 percent of subjects confronted successfully.

CHALLENGING CONVERSATIONS SUCCESS RATE

Figure 3: General approaches to Challenging Conversations

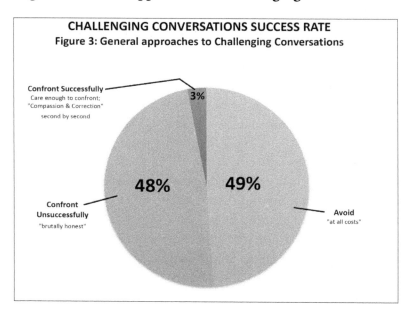

CHALLENGING CONVERSATIONS SUCCESS RATE
Figure 3: General approaches to Challenging Conversations

Confront Successfully
Care enough to confront;
"Compassion & Correction"
second by second

3%

48%   49%

Confront
Unsuccessfully
"brutally honest"

Avoid
"at all costs"

Two additional points seem worthy of highlighting. Being brutally honest is probably the simplest explanation why 48 percent of the sample failed to confront successfully. It is argued strongly that there is no place for brutality in any relationship, whether personal or professional. Only 3 percent of the sample demonstrated courage sufficiently to confront but did so with a caring approach involving respect and love.

Why challenging conversations are difficult

The data collected and reported above initially stunned me, and I struggled to look for explanations. I began by first acknowledging the widely respected work behind the popular behavioural profile known as the DiSC® Assessment, based on the DiSC® theory of psychologist William Moulton Marston. Involving over 40 million people in the sample, this tool is designed to give an understanding to behavioural differences between people regardless of age, gender, or cultural background. Participants can be seen to have a dominance in at least one of the following clusters of behaviours with associated priorities, motivations, and approaches to others:

- D: Dominance – the driver type. "Get it done."
- I: Influence – the expressive type. "Get it recognized."
- S: Steadiness – the amiable type. "Get along."
- C: Conscientiousness – the analytical type. "Get it right."

Research shows that both the "S" and the "C" styles have considerable difficulty with managing challenging conversations, and simply prefer to avoid them rather than deal with potential conflict.

That portion of the world therefore tends naturally to avoid challenging conversations. While significant, this doesn't really explain why such conversations are so difficult. While revealing observations, the data are not explanatory.

Patterson et al. attempted to address the *why* question. They offered an explanation by reporting that they believe people—including leaders—are what they call "designed wrong."

They poignantly remind us that countless generations of genetic shaping drove humans to handle challenging conversations with flying fists and fleet feet, not intelligent persuasion and gentle intelligence. When someone says something you strongly disagree with about a topic that matters a great deal to you, your adrenal glands pump adrenalin into your bloodstream. You don't choose to do this, your adrenal glands do it, and then you have to take the consequences.

Furthermore, your brain then diverts blood from what it deems non-essential activities to high-priority ones, such as hitting and running. Unfortunately, as the larger muscles of the arms and legs get more blood, the higher-level reasoning sections of our bodies receive less. The result is that physiologically you end up facing a challenging conversation with mental equipment equivalent to that of a gorilla.

Furthermore, when we are under pressure we spontaneously say things that later on make us wonder *What on earth was I thinking?* The reality is that we often wing a challenging conversation while multiprocessing with a half-starved brain. The result is that we often use our worst behaviour within circumstances that matter most to us. Thus, self-defeating behaviours are most commonly associated with challenging conversations.

For example, you are increasingly irritated by your new hire not putting equipment and files back where you think they belong. You start nagging her about cleaning up. She starts nagging you about your nagging. The more the two of you push each other, the more you create the very behaviours that each of you despise. This example is merely the tip of an enormous iceberg of problems which evolve from potentially challenging conversations having been avoided or gone wrong.

Other examples of topics that could easily lead to disastrous outcomes include

- giving the boss feedback on his behaviour.
- approaching a boss who is breaking his own safety or quality policies.
- resolving custody issues with an ex-spouse.
- talking to a colleague who is hoarding resources or information.

- giving an unfavourable performance review.
- talking to a team member about a hygiene problem.

Another key reason why challenging conversations are difficult and why only 3 percent of my 7,082 leaders successfully resolved their challenging conversations is because a successful outcome necessitates that the people involved strive for *dialogue*, not *discussion*. This is far from easy for most of us. Worthy of note is the observation that the term *discussion* comes from the Latin root *percussio*, which translates into English as "a forcible striking of one object against another," as in the terms *percussion* and *concussion*. If your boss tells you to "come into my office, I have something to *discuss* with you," you can safely conclude that you are in trouble and should probably be prepared psychologically to duck. The term *dialogue*, in contrast, involves the exchange of ideas without judgment, so caring is its basis, not condemnation or a forcible striking of one idea/person against another.

Leaders skilled at dialogue make it safe for everyone present to add their viewpoint and value to the shared pool, including ideas that at first impression may appear wrong, controversial, or at odds with the majority. The successful leader probably won't agree with everyone but may ensure that all ideas find their way into the "pool of shared meaning," as Patterson et al. call it. It is a measure of the group's IQ. The larger the pool, the smarter the decision. Where there is an open and free exchange of ideas, the increased time investment is more than offset by the quality of the decision. The pool of shared meaning becomes the birthplace of synergy and carefree conversation.

In comparison, when the pool is dangerously shallow, "people purposefully withhold meaning from one another, individually smart people can do collectively stupid things."[34]

For example, a woman checked into the hospital to have a tonsillectomy and the surgical team erroneously removed a portion of her foot. How could this tragedy happen? In fact, why is it that ninety-eight-thousand hospital deaths each year stem from human error?[35] In part, it is because many health-care professionals are afraid to speak their minds. In this case, no less than seven people wondered why the surgeon was working on the foot but said nothing. Wisdom did not prevail because people were afraid to speak up.

Of course, hospitals don't have a monopoly on fear. In every instance where bosses are smart, highly paid, confident, and outspoken (i.e., most of the world), people tend to hold back their opinions rather than risk angering someone in a position of power.

When people aren't involved, when they sit back quietly during touchy conversations, they're rarely committed to the final decision. Since their ideas remain in their heads and their opinions never make it into the pool, they end up quietly criticizing and passively resisting. Worse still, when others force their ideas into the pool, people have a harder time accepting the information. They may *say* they're on board, but then walk away and follow through half-heartedly. To quote Samuel Butler, "He that complies against his will is of his own opinion still."[36]

Every time we find ourselves arguing, debating, running away, or otherwise acting in an ineffective way, it's because we don't know how to share meaning. Instead of engaging in healthy dialogue, we play silly and costly games.

For instance, sometimes we move to silence. We play "salute and stay mute." That is, we don't confront people in positions of authority. At home we may play "freeze your lover." With this tortured technique we give loved ones the cold shoulder in order to get them to treat us better—totally illogical.

Sometimes we rely on hints, sarcasm, innuendo, and looks of disgust to make our points. We play the martyr and then pretend we're actually trying to help. Afraid to confront an individual, we blame an entire team for a problem, hoping the message will hit the right target. Whatever the technique, the overall method is the same. We withhold meaning from the pool. We go to silence.

On other occasions, not knowing how to stay in dialogue we may rely on violence—anything from subtle manipulation to verbal attacks. We act like we know everything, hoping people will believe our arguments. We discredit others, hoping people won't believe their arguments. And then we use every manner of force to get our way. We borrow power from the boss; we hit people with biased monologues. The goal, of course, is always the same: to compel others to our point of view.

Caring sufficiently to confront another involves starting a challenging conversation with an open heart. Begin a high-risk conversation with the right motives and stay focused no matter what happens. You maintain focus by

1. knowing exactly what you really want. Despite constant temptations and invitations to slip away from your goals, stick with them.
2. avoiding making "either/or" choices. Unlike those who justify their unhealthy behaviour by claiming that they had no choice but to fight or take flight, the caring stance maintains that dialogue is always an option.

Here's a summary of why so few leaders truly succeed when faced with challenging conversations:

- Bad leaders edit the truth for fear of causing discomfort.
- Good leaders accept that the truth is often uncomfortable.
- Great leaders value the truth and confront the discomfort by seeing it as an opportunity to rise above the difficulty involved.

Popular, but inadequately detailed templates for challenging conversations

Figure 4: Popular Challenging Conversation Model

1. **Communicate the issue.**
   I want to talk to you about how _____
   is affecting _____

2. **Give recent and specific examples of the behaviour(s).**
   For example: _____

3. **Articulate your emotional response to this issue.**
   I feel _____

4. **Share why this is important to you, to the team, to the client(s), etc.**
   This is very important because _____

5. **Be accountable by sharing how you may be contributing to this issue. Apologize (if applicable).**
   I recognize that I may have contributed to this issue by _____

6. **Genuine interest to solve the problem.**
   Together I want to solve this issue of _____

7. **Listen to the other person.**
   Please help me to understand your perspective on this issue.

Figure 5: Challenging Conversation Model (Example)

This example represents a challenging conversation with an employee who has been frequently late for work.

1. **Communicate the issue.**
   I want to talk to you about your frequent lateness is affecting our productivity here at the office.

2. **Give recent and specific examples of the behaviour(s).**
   For example, last Friday you arrived at 9:10 a.m., and this past Tuesday, you were late coming back to the office after lunch by thirty minutes.

3. **Articulate your emotional response to the issue.**
   I feel frustrated and disappointed.

4. **Share why this is important to you, to the team, to the client(s), etc.**
   This is very important because our productivity suffers. On Friday I had one hour available for our staff meeting, and when you arrived forty minutes late, we had only twenty minutes to discuss these important matters. It is important in that you are setting an example for others, and it is important that you be available when our clients phone or come into our office.

5. **Be accountable by sharing how you may be contributing to this issue. Apologize.**
   I recognize that I may have contributed to this issue in that I have chosen not to address this on numerous occasions, and I may have given the impression this may not be very important. I am sorry.

6. **Genuine interest to solve the problem.**
   Together I want to solve this issue of how your lateness is impacting myself, other team members and our clients.

7. **Listen to the other person.**
   Please help me to understand your perspective on this issue.

Harvard Project with example of Peter and Sue

Let's look at an example in order to acknowledge the need to listen "between the lines" when in dialogue.

Peter picks up a voice message from his fiancée, Sue, who ended the conversation with, "I love you, but why the heck are you always at the office?"

Concerned, Peter decides to surprise Sue with a pair of expensive front-row tickets to Mozart's opera *The Magic Flute*, because he knows she loves opera and he will have to leave the office early to be able to take her out to a nice restaurant before the concert. He even leaves earlier than he wanted to in order to surprise her on his way home the next day.

He brings flowers and taps on her door at 5:00 p.m.

Sue: "Oh, hi, I wasn't expecting you. Why aren't you at the office?"

Peter: "I left early to see you and give you a surprise gift."

Sue: "Gift? Come in."

Peter: [handing her the flowers] "Thanks. Hope you like them."

Sue: "Thanks, but you know I don't like orchids in this colour. Don't you remember we changed my wedding dress so it wouldn't be this colour? Anyway, thanks. How's work?"

Peter: "Oh, fine. It's really busy, but hey, I left early to bring you these [hands her the opera tickets]. I think it's your favourite."

Sue: [opens envelope] "Oh, Peter! *The Magic Flute!* Wow! [looks closer at the tickets] Oh heck, you really screwed up on this one. That's Mum's birthday, and you know she expects us to be at her place for the evening."

Peter: "But this is for you, not your mother."

Sue: "How could you possibly be so mean?"

Peter: "OK. Give 'em back. I'll change them to another night."

Sue: "I know you're busy, but I'm sure you'll fix it. It would be a disaster to upset Mum."

Peter: "Sure. I have to go now, but I'll call you tomorrow. 'Bye."

Now let's look more deeply at what words were said, what meanings Peter heard, and his resultant feelings and identity, from Peter's perspective only.

What Peter and Sue actually said	What Peter actually thought and felt, but didn't say
Sue: "I love you, but why the heck are you always at the office?"	*Damnit! Don't you know I'll have to be the breadwinner?*
Sue: "Oh, hi, I wasn't expecting you. Why aren't you at the office?" Peter: "I left early to see you to give you a surprise gift."	
	When will she stop complaining? I busted my rear end to be here and surprise her. Is that all the appreciation I get?

Sue: "Gift? Come in." Peter: "Thanks. Hope you like them."	
	She'd better say a big thank you
Sue: "Thanks, but you know I don't like orchids this colour. Don't you remember we changed my wedding dress so it wouldn't be this colour?"	
	A total overreaction! Anyway, she should know I'm colour blind. At the same time, I'm angry at myself for messing up here. I should have asked the florist what colour they were.
Sue: "Anyway, thanks. How's work?"	
	As if she cares! Ungrateful woman. I'm angry.
Peter: "Oh, fine. It's really busy, but hey, I left early to bring you these. I think it's your favourite."	
	She'd better like this. After all, they were $300.

Sue: "Oh, Peter! *The Magic Flute.* Wow!"	
	At last. Maybe I'll end up OK after all.
Sue: "Oh heck, you really screwed up on this one. That's Mum's birthday, and you know she expects us to be at her place for the evening."	
	Damn it! I messed up again.
Peter: But this is for you, not your mother.	
	Get your priorities straight, dummy.
Sue: How could you be so mean?	
	Oh, here we go again . . . the mother-in-law issue. I'm ticked off with her.
Peter: OK. Give 'em back. I'll change them to another night.	
	Grrr. Bite your tongue, stupid.

Sue: I know you're busy, but I'm sure you'll fix it. It would be a disaster to upset Mum.	
	Man alive! I wish your meddling mum would bloody disappear. I'm so pissed. I wish she'd kick the bucket.
Peter: Sure. I have to go now, but I'll call you tomorrow. 'Bye.	
	I'm out of here!

Summary

Chapter 2 presents a brief review of the most popular literature currently available on the topic of challenging conversations.

Data from the author's own survey of over 7,000 business leaders around the world showed that 49 percent of the sample generally chose to avoid challenging conversations at all costs, while 48 percent chose to confront but believe that being brutality honest is an appropriate element in confronting another. Thus, two conclusions become evident: (1) the latter 48 percent of leaders failed to resolve their differences satisfactorily, as it is argued that there is no place for brutality in any relationship, whether personal or professional. (2) Only 3 percent of leaders demonstrated the courage to confront, but did so with a caring approach, which facilitated a mutually satisfactory resolution. These data have profound implications, and most certainly show the extreme importance of the topic and the need to address it directly.

A partial explanation for these potentially alarming results was offered by using the well-respected behavioural profile known as DiSC®, which identifies a classification system that allows people of all races, ages, and cultural backgrounds to be described as predominantly one of four types: dominance, influence, steadiness, or conscientiousness. Extensive research by the authors show that the conscientiousness and steadiness groupings tend to be particularly uncomfortable with conflict and so tend to avoid challenging conversations. The other half of the world tend to confront, but often fail to do so satisfactorily.

Physiological explanations are part of this human failing, but the chapter also points to the inadequacy of the most common approaches published today.

Points to Ponder

1. Think of a real person with whom you have had a personally challenging conversation. Record what words were stated and what you actually thought and felt but did not say. Use the same two columns as illustrated with the Peter and Sue example.
2. Similarly record a conversation you have experienced with another person within your work world.

Chapter 3

Higher-Level Caring Model

A pilot who wishes to fly to New York must first know whether the plane is currently standing in Toronto, London, or Chicago.

As this axiom reminds us, the prerequisite to moving forward is to know exactly where we currently stand. Therefore, in order to climb to a higher level, let's review the current widely accepted level of recommended techniques to handle challenging conversations.

The recorded number of hits and the nodding heads of the worldwide audience suggest that a recent TEDx Talk on the topic of challenging conversations typifies and affirms the current level of understanding, as well as research findings published globally.

In her talk entitled "Coming Out of Your Closet,"[37] Ash Beckham acknowledges the importance of caring enough to confront. She points out that we all have closets—not necessarily in the traditional sense, but telling someone you're pregnant or that you have cancer, or that you love them, are all examples of what she terms a "closet." "All a closet is, is a hard conversation. It's hard, it's scary, and it needs to be done carefully."

The main reason a conversation—such as telling your partner that you've just gone bankrupt—is challenging because you worry about how the other person will react. Will they be angry, disappointed, hurt? Will we lose a friend, a parent, a lover? Worry causes stress and stress causes sickness and shorter lives. If you don't throw the grenade, it will kill you.

Beckham urges the listener to (1) be authentic, (2) be direct, and (3) be unapologetic. As the famous Nike advertisement suggests, just do it!

But this approach is too simplistic and does little to help people deal successfully with challenging conversations. If it was as easy as one-two-three, Beckman suggests, we wouldn't have 97 percent of people around the world essentially failing at this critical skill. There is a blatant need to move to a higher level in order to improve, and an excellent beginning point is spelled out by leadership experts and authors Jim Kouzes and Barry Posner.

In their respected text *The Leadership Challenge*,[38] they devote a chapter to "encouraging the heart." They argue that caring unconditionally is the fundamental beginning point of a successfully conducted challenging conversation, and that the "best kept secret of successful leaders is love: being in love with leading, with the people who do the work. Leadership is an affair of the heart, not the head."

Vince Lombardi, the renowned former coach of the Green Bay Packers, similarly stated that a challenging conversation must start with a loving heart; in fact, unconditional love. He argued that caring was best described as love. In a speech he delivered to the American Management Association, he stated:

> Mental toughness to humility, simplicity, separatism, and love. I don't necessarily have to like my associates, but as a person I have to love them. Love respects the ambiguity of the other individual. Heart-power is the strength of any corporation.

These are such easy words to express with our tongue and lips, but amazingly difficult to demonstrate with our actions.

Much of the world will know the Beatles work "All You Need Is Love," and may even be familiar with John Mayer's more recent reminder that "Love is a Verb." Love is an action, an act of will, rather than feeling.

But how well are we doing?

The disturbing reality is that divorce, family dysfunction, violence, and abuse are characteristics of these modern times.

All of these communication breakdowns, even wars, can be traced back to people's inability to deal with the differences between one another. Too quickly we slip into defending our ego or our viewpoint by judging the others' as wrong and worthy only of condemnation: not worthy of listening to in order to understand.

If we really see love as a verb and attempt to care enough to confront, we have to begin with a commitment to dropping judgment.

The modern times referred to above puts us in mind of the well-known title of one of Charlie Chaplin's most famous films. He made the movie in 1936, four years before he created *The Great Dictator*, which contains the following from Chaplin's final speech:

> I don't want to rule and conquer anyone. I should like to help people—Jewish, Gentile, black man, white. We want to live by each other's happiness, not by each other's misery. We don't want to hate and despise one another. But we have lost the way. Greed has poisoned men's souls; has barricaded the world with hate . . . More than machinery, we need humanity. More than cleverness we need kindness and generosity. Without these qualities, life will be violent and will be lost. The misery that is now upon us is but greed, the bitterness of men. Only the unloved hate; the unloved and the unnatural. In the seventeenth chapter of St. Luke, it is written that the kingdom of God is

within man, not one man nor a group of men, but all men!

How much have we learned since this speech in 1940?

The distressing answer is …not much. It is intimately connected with the human tendency to judge and condemn rather than listen and seek in order to demonstrate sufficient caring—at least to listen and share without judgment. The news regarding the death of George Floyd is testament to our not having learned much since 1940.

Grasping the fundamental difference between *discussion* and *dialogue* is an effective beginning point.

The Oxford dictionary defines *discussion* as "an examination by argument." We need, however, to recognize that the Latin root of discussion, *percussio*, means a "forcible striking of one object against another." The word *percussion* is reserved for the orchestra player who forcibly beats the skins of his drums. Similarly, *concussion* involves a severe striking of one's skull to knock us senseless.

As noted earlier in this chapter, when a supervisor invites an employee to "step into my office, I have something to discuss with you," the employee can accurately predict that he'd better be prepared to duck. Forcible striking of the boss's viewpoint against the employee's can be anticipated as the fundamental paradigm from which the boss is operating. The supervisor in this case is actually using the term *discussion* ironically, rather than the truthful "I want to lecture you."

Chances are far too high that the result will be a disempowered employee, and this can easily be the start of the chain of behaviours that include feeling disrespected, then hurt, then angry, then resentful, then rebellious, then stealing or breaking ethical boundaries in order to get even.

An employee who winds up feeling abused by this discussion paradigm will predictably spread poisonous gossip and foster rebellion. The challenging conversation between Inspector Javert and Jean Valjean at the beginning of the musical *Les Misérables*, where the discussion paradigm is dominant, predictably leads to ultimate rebellion and resultant loss of lives.

The Oxford dictionary defines *dialogue* as "a conversation or exchange of ideas where judgment of the other is dropped."

The difference between *discussion* and *dialogue* dramatically portrays the difference between the second and third choice we have in dealing with challenging conversations.

We can

1. avoid.
2. handle unsuccessfully.
3. handle successfully.

To envision even the hope of advancement to a higher level, we need to see unconditional love as the underpinning to any challenging conversation that is going to end with the parties involved being mutually content with the resolution.

Conditional love simply means that love, caring, and acceptance are withheld until certain conditions are fulfilled. For example, the parent who withholds affection for her daughter until she drops her boyfriend is setting up a scenario where the daughter will likely leave home and break contact from her "unloving" mother.

Caring (loving) enough to confront necessitates demonstrating caring without conditions.

While uncommon, the skills underpinning unconditional love are easy to identify and relatively easy to learn. As Patterson points out in his "Today's Handling of Effective Conversation":

> First consider the fact that a well-handled crucial conversation all but leaps out at you. In fact, when you see someone enter the dangerous waters of a

high-stakes, high-emotion controversial conversation and the person does a particularly good job, your natural reaction is to step back in awe. "Wow" is generally the first word out of your mouth. What starts as a doomed discussion ends up with a healthy resolution. It can take your breath away.

As long as we adopt a paradigm of caring and unconditional love, we can transform challenging conversations from frightening events into interactions which yield successful, enriching results.

However, it has to be recognized that we cannot simply drink a potion of "caring" and walk away renewed. Instead, the renewing of the mind begins by taking a long, hard, honest look at your own heart. Just as leadership comes from within and boils down to a disposition more than a position, successfully dealing with challenging conversations comes from within you, the reader.

The words of Mary Solum[39] have touched me ever since I faced death at 8,000 feet and gained profound insights when I first had to face Kathleen and come to grips with the nature of challenging conversations:

> I have come to a frightful conclusion. I am the decisive element in the organization. It is my personal leadership and daily mood that creates the climate, the culture. It is my daily mood that makes the weather. As a leader, I possess tremendous power to make a person's life miserable or joyous. I can be an instrument of torture, or an instrument of inspiration. I can humiliate or humour. I can hurt or heal. In all situations it is my response that determines whether a crisis will be escalated or de-escalated, a person humanized or de-humanized.
>
> The New Leader[40]

The powerful and profound implications which fall from this conclusion is that choice is our greatest freedom, and we *can* turn a difficult conversation into healing and resolution if we fully accept the "frightening" conclusion that Solum identifies. There appears to be a high probability that Solum modified words originally written by Haim Ginott,[41] so I take the liberty again to paraphrase her words:

> I have come to a frightening conclusion. I am the decisive element in any challenging conversation. It is my daily leadership and choosing to love unconditionally that enable me to live with faith, hope, and love . . . but it has to be unconditional.

I can easily fool myself, or look deeply into my ego; I can easily defend myself or acknowledge my vulnerability; I can hurt or heal; perceive challenge as a gift or reason to quit; another's obnoxious behaviour as a cry for help, or excuse to retaliate.

It all begins with me and my readiness to take the high road, adopt unconditional love or become sucked into the valley of bitterness which leads only to a self-imposed cage of limitations.

Perhaps the seminal work leading to acknowledging thought choice as our greatest freedom is that of James Allen, who, back in 1902, wrote in *As a Man Thinketh*:[42]

> A person cannot directly choose his circumstances, but he can choose his thoughts, and so indirectly yet surely shape his circumstances.

Twin brothers illustrate the significance of Allen's work and its crucial relevance to how we approach any challenging conversation. One boy grows up to be an alcoholic bum, the other grows up to be a very successful business leader. When the alcoholic is asked why he became a drunk, he replies, "My father was a drunk." When the successful businessman is asked why he became successful, he replies, "My father was a drunk."

Same background. Same upbringing. Very different choice.

We either live in the problem or in the solution. It boils down to our individual thought choice. The simple but profound truth is that you are today where your thoughts brought you, as you will tomorrow be where your thoughts take you.

As Allen stated over a hundred years ago:

> A person is literally what he thinks, his character
> being the complete sum of all his thoughts.[43]

Good thoughts and actions can never produce bad results. Bad thoughts and actions can never produce good results. Thus, higher-level thoughts of love and caring for a person with whom you experience conflict cannot produce bad outcomes.

If hateful and condemnatory thoughts arise in challenging conversations, they crystallize into actions and habits of accusation and violence, which solidify into circumstances of injury and persecution. Selfish thoughts crystallize into habits of self-seeking, which solidify into stressful circumstances.

On the other hand, and on a higher level of caring, beautiful, loving thoughts crystallize into habits of grace and kindliness, which solidify into genial and positive circumstances.

- I must rule my mind or it will rule me.
- It's not what you think I am; it's what I think... I am.
- Thought choice is my freedom, my responsibility, my power, the determinant of my success.
- I must be very careful what I think, and as my mother used to say, "Be careful what you pray for. You'll get it."

Summary

This chapter argues that the "just do it" attitude toward a challenging conversation is grossly inadequate, and it emphasizes how important our own thought choices are. We become what we think; therefore, we should choose beforehand to adopt an unconditionally caring attitude of love. The resulting conversation is thus going to evolve as *dialogue* rather than *discussion*, because it is characterized by the absence of judgment. The renewing of the mind begins by taking a long, hard, honest look at your own heart. Successfully dealing with a challenging conversation comes from you.

The simple but profound truth is that you are today where your thoughts brought you, as you will tomorrow be where your thoughts take you.

Points to Ponder

Find a quiet place to reflect and return to the examples of challenging conversations you noted at the end of Chapter 1. Be honest and consider the following:

1. List the lovable characteristics of the other participant in the conversation.
2. Remembering that their obnoxious behaviour is most likely simply a cry for help. How are they hurting?
3. Seeing their obnoxious behaviour as an opportunity for you to be of assistance rather than an excuse to retaliate, what could you do for them?
4. What do they need most?
5. Will you forgive them?
6. How have you contributed to the tension between you?

If you cannot honestly answer these questions, is it best to leave the relationship, position, or situation? And if you draw a blank on all these questions, is it because you cannot or will not?

The remainder of the text presents the following ABCs of moving to higher ground when dealing successfully with challenging conversations.

- Section A comprises fundamentals of **A**ttitude.
- Section B comprises fundamentals of **B**ehaviour.
- Section C comprises fundamentals of **C**aring.

SECTION A: ATTITUDE

CHOOSING TO SEE CHALLENGING CONVERSATIONS AS GIFTS IN DISGUISE

Chapter 4

Shattering the Glass Ceiling of Our Thinking

Mindset separates the best from rest.

— Denis Shackel

Our present success level at dealing with challenging conversations is simply the effects of our current beliefs, mental state, and daily habits. Most fear is simply bad management of the mind.

When our goals and aspirations are not aligned with our current mental set and habits, we become stuck, filled with doubts and procrastination. Something within you has to change before your current habits will change.

We've been conditioned to think in the same way and exhibit the same behaviours repeatedly. This maintains our current results, known as the Comfort Zone, and also maintains our current level of success in dealing with challenging conversations.

The Comfort Zone is potentially a very dangerous place, as all can easily become stuck to the same behaviours. Our own brain makes us stuck! Fear of failure, low self-esteem, lack of certainty, not trusting yourself . . . these are all effects of thought choice.

Peter Senge[44] eloquently describes the "creative tension" between a person's desired future state and current reality—his Comfort Zone—by means of the following diagram involving a stretched rubber band:

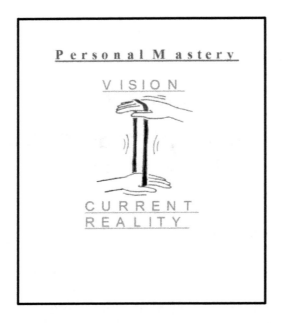

Research findings show that the majority (probably 97 percent) of the world deal with the tension between their current reality and desired dream by giving up the dream. The best (3 percent) separate themselves from the rest by fixing their attention, focus, and commitment on the dream, and experience their current reality rising to that goal. The practical implications for all of us dealing with challenging conversations, especially those in leadership positions, is clear. We have a profound choice between more of the same or more of the new.

The reframing of thinking physiologically involves sending blood to the thinking centre as opposed to the anxiety centre. But first, let's look at the brain:

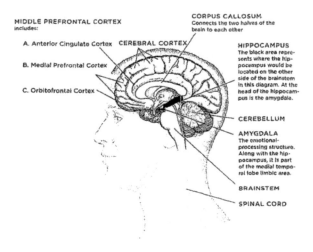

Centres of the Brain

To reach a higher level of dealing with challenging conversations, we need simply to retrain the brain. The rapidly developing field of neuroscience offers techniques to accomplish this reframing and actual creation of new, constructive neural pathways to overcoming fear, which results from constrictive neural patterns.

Recent and revolutionary work proving we can change our minds, brains, fears, and relationships is being led by researchers and their works, such as:

- Daniel Siegel, *Mindsight: The New Science of Personal Transformation*[45]
- Norman Doidge, *The Brain that Changes Itself*[46]
- Jill Bolte Taylor, *My Stroke of Insight*[47]

Dr. Srini Pillay is another leader bringing contemporary neuroscience to the everyday life of challenging conversations. Pillay[48] removes the veil from the mysteries of the interface between mind, brain, and relationships between people in both professional and personal settings. His model is a focused attention that allows us to see the inner working of our own mind. It enables us to be aware of our mental processes without being swept away by them, which helps us to get off the autopilot of ingrained, habitual responses and moves us beyond the reactive emotional blocks that we all have a tendency to be trapped within.

Fear is fear of emotions, not fear of the event.

For example, fear of public speaking is not really fear of the event, but fear of being embarrassed, ashamed, or inadequate. Therefore, Pillay's five-step technique to overcome fear of challenging conversations allows us to name and tame the emotions we are feeling when confronting a difficult interaction.

Consider the difference between "I am angry" and "I feel angry." Similar as those two statements may seem, there is actually a profound difference between them. "I am angry" is a self-definition, and a very limiting one. "I feel angry" involves the ability to recognize a feeling, but without being consumed by it. The five-step technique involves thought choices that make it possible to see inside our emotions and to accept them, and in the accepting to let them go without judgment, which finally transforms them.

Fear causes stress which physiologically increases the flow of blood to the anxiety centre of the brain (the *amygdala*, see diagram above). This in turn takes blood from the frontal cortex and so impacts the thinking centre of our brains. Our whole decision-making system is therefore crippled.

Dr. Pillay has published five steps to enable us to deactivate the anxiety centre and activate the thinking centre. Based on eighteen years of research at Harvard University involving thousands of subjects, he has proven the effectiveness of what he refers to as the "CIRCA" approach to overcoming fear and thus handle challenging conversations successfully.

CIRCA stands for the following five steps:

1. Chunking
2. Ignore your fear-fuelled thoughts
3. Reality check
4. Control check
5. Attention shift

Chunking

Chunking is breaking down big goals to smaller, manageable ones. When I was facing death at 8,000 feet, as described in *Five Seconds at a Time*, I stepped back, paused, and rather than become totally overwhelmed with the crisis I was facing, broke the seemingly impossible task of surviving eight hours of minus 30-degree temperatures into smaller bites of manageable periods, namely, five second intervals.

I now know from Pillay's research that this first step simply moved blood from my anxiety centre (amygdala) to where I needed it: my thinking centre (cerebral cortex).

By way of example, an employee—let's call him Steve—has an issue with his aggressive boss, Roger. Rather than become overwhelmed with the enormity of confronting the boss with the brutality of the boss's unwarranted bullying behaviour (and probability end up being fired), Steve chunks the challenging conversation down to a manageable opening question, such as, "Roger, can we talk in private about something that is really bothering me?" You can safely predict that the answer will be yes, which can then lead to a statement such as, "Thank you. I do have something to talk with you about that I think will help us work together more effectively."

Ignore your fear-fuelled thoughts

Do you find it difficult fully to relax? Does your head seem full of thoughts swirling around your brain so intensely that you can't sleep? Has your head ached with countless thoughts bombarding you with their cacophony of internal voices?

I suspect we can all identify with these experiences and times when we are internally "out of breath."

Ignoring your fear-fuelled thoughts, your mental chatter, simply involves placing the intentional brain's flashlight on your breathing. The best definition of anxiety I have ever come across is from Fritz Perls (father of Gestalt therapy, a form of psychotherapy focusing on personal responsibility) who defined it as "excitement without breath."[49]

Simply pausing and focusing on your breaths, and even counting them—"one, two, three, four, five"—is a well-documented technique to flow blood from your anxiety to your thinking centre. Yoga around the world acknowledges this technique as a profoundly simple yet effective means to cease the mental chatter.

This of course is basically the title of my book *Five Seconds at a Time*. I focused on a single breath for each five-second period. This saved my life. I have bone-marrow conviction that I did not get through eight hours of 30-below temperatures while wearing very little clothing in one long stretch. I don't think that would be possible. All I did was get through eight hours of minus-30-degree temperatures for five seconds, for one breath, and then did it again. I did this 5,760 times, one breath at a time.

Similarly, the mental chatter associated with confronting a challenging conversation can be successfully eliminated by counting your breaths. My extreme anxiety in confronting Kathleen was largely dealt with when we both experienced our breathing. When we initially embraced, both shaking uncontrollably with tears and emotional devastation, neither of us could talk. It was only when our breathing became in synch with each other that we could communicate.

My internal chatter as I was helped out of the helicopter and assisted to meet Kathleen was chatter I will never forget. My internal list of questions, concerns, doubts, fears, and catastrophic expectations were amongst the highest I have ever experienced in my life.

I now find it an illumination to realize that our challenging conversation began only when our breathing harmonized and blood began to activate my cerebral cortex's thinking centre. I began to manage the chatter and emotional trauma only when I focused my brain's flashlight on my breathing.

Reality check

In its simplest form, this step involves choosing to fill your brain with thoughts best described as "this too will pass." This is helpful when you are feeling caught up in a bombardment of questions, things like *How can I raise the $200,000 I need? What if the bank won't give me the mortgage? Can my weak heart possibly handle the effects of the chemotherapy?* When you feel out of control, simply reading "this too will pass" out loud from a sticky note you can place on the fridge sends blood to where it is needed and calms you down.

When stranded at 8,000 feet facing death, the reality check I found particularly reassuring was the knowledge that Kathleen would definitely alert the authorities about Bruce and me not arriving at the planned time. The certainty of knowing she would sound the alarm and arrange a rescue party at dawn enabled me to recognize in my thinking centre that even this, the longest night of my life, would pass. I clearly recall that this reality check led automatically to seeing the night as already passed, as represented by my vision of seeing the rising sun. It was the reality check which enabled me to envision that too passing.

Control check

This fourth step of CIRCA involves the three-step process of

1. figuring out what you can control
2. figuring out what you cannot control, and
3. recognizing the things you cannot control and letting them go by giving them up.

The Serenity Prayer, first credited to American theologian Reinhold Niebuhr,[50] sums this up beautifully:

> God, grant me the serenity to accept the things
> I cannot change, courage to change the things I
> can, and wisdom to know the difference.

Control check is primarily about giving up the things that you cannot control. This is a central underpinning to successful challenging conversations. Remember, you cannot change the person with whom you have an emotionally charged difference. The only person you can change is yourself, which implies the truth that in challenging conversations the mental paradigm the leader must adopt is not *How can I change the other person?* but *How can I change in order that the other person changes their behaviour?* Rather than ask *How can I control the ocean?* ask *How can I surf the wave?*

The life-changing night on the mountain was a profoundly spiritual experience.

Initially, I heard the words of Philippians 4:13: "I can do all things through Christ who strengthens me" while I was still outside of the hut, wondering how I was going to be able to scale the ice wall. Then I discovered the identical message when turning to the Gideon Bible, which "happened" to be there in the hut. All of this gave me an amazing sense of peace and an ability to breathe deeper than before. At the time, I experienced this as an overwhelming sense of God's grace, but now, several years later, I gain yet another illumination.

Yes, I knew the Serenity Prayer on the night of May 17, 1997, and yes, it was probably influencing my mental state, at least on a subconscious level, but what I have discovered since beginning my research on the topic of challenging conversations is that the full verse of the Serenity Prayer has extra elements interwoven in the second verse. I now see that it explains my life-changing experience even more fully. Here is Reinhold Niebuhr's full version, which I discovered years after the longest night of my life.

> God, give me the grace to accept with serenity
> the things that cannot be changed,
> Courage to change the things
> which should be changed,
> and the wisdom to distinguish
> the one from the other.
>
> Living one day at a time,
> Enjoying one moment at a time,
> Accepting hardship as a pathway to peace,
> Taking, as Christ did,
> This sinful world as it is,
> Not as I would have it,
> Trusting that You will make all things right,
> If I surrender to Your will,
> So that I may be reasonably happy in this life,
> And supremely happy with You forever in the next.
>
> Amen.

It is worth repeating that facing death at 8,000 feet was a deeply spiritual experience. Yet, as stated on page 17 of *Five Seconds at a Time*:

> My story and lessons learned are personal and disclose beliefs largely of a spiritual nature, which do not generally appear in texts on leadership, influence, power or business success. My intention is not to manipulate or convert readers to my particular belief system. However, I have become convinced that leadership is a journey towards integrity, a holistic unison of body, mind, and soul, and therefore, a spiritual journey.

I am equally prepared to acknowledge the spiritual component involved in caring enough, in loving enough, to confront another person in a challenging conversation. Furthermore, seriously studying the field of challenging conversations has intensified my conviction that a leader is a custodian of the human spirit, and challenging conversations are dealt with successfully only when we adopt the higher ground of love.

My readiness to acknowledge prayer as a key to dealing successfully with challenging conversations underlies Pillay's control check.

Attention shift

In recent years I have become convinced that where your attention goes, energy flows.

When your amygdala is activated by stress and blood flows to that anxiety centre of the brain, your attention tends to go to it, and all you see is threat. It focuses on self-hatred, self-shame, and negative qualities of yourself. And it focuses on what most commonly causes the derailment of challenging conversations: the negative qualities of the other person.

However, the frontal cortex (an even more powerful part of the brain) has power to redirect flashlight focus back on the solutions. Neurologically, this is a simple shift from *problem focus* to *solution focus*. This does not mean that you necessarily know the solution before you begin the challenging conversation, but it at least turns on the *possibility brain*; i.e., it gives your conscious brain permission to tell your unconscious brain that it needs to figure something out. This may sound only theoretical, but in fact it is very practical. When you are stuck in the anxiety centre, your brain can't really figure anything out.

This "flashlight" simply asks the unconscious mind, *What is the solution?* With the right sort of brain talk you can change what's going on in your brain.

That's certainly what enabled me to survive the phenomenal cold of May 17, and what will enable you to move into the elite 3 percent of leaders who successfully handle challenging conversations.

During my mountain ordeal I was aware of innumerable times when fears of dying and not seeing the rising sun, or thoughts of survival being impossible, would creep into my mind. All I did was refocus on what I wanted and not what I didn't want, and redirect the flashlight to the vision of seeing dawn—to not failing to see the rising sun—and I self-talked my way to focus on the goal, not the obstacles.

Furthermore, the whole experience powerfully taught me that an obstacle is simply what you see when you take your eyes off the goal or vision.

- Was this easy? No, of course not.
- Is leadership easy? No, of course not!
- Is handling challenging conversations easy? No, of course not.

An additional conclusion is the belief that self-discipline is the underpinning to successful leadership. No one really wants to be managed if the experience of being managed is a sense of loss of control or freedom. Manage yourself with self-discipline and you will be able to lead others.

The self-discipline of attention shift saved my life. The self-discipline of managing self is the key to successful challenging conversations.

Paradoxes abound!

- The key to human influence is to first be influenced.
- The key to effective leadership is first to manage yourself.
- The key to solving challenging conversations is first to change your behaviour.

It is now time to come to grips with the crucial importance of practice, practice, practice in order to establish neural circuits in your brain which fire automatically to facilitate your rising to the top 3 percent.

Habit formation: Retrain your brain

When neurons fire together, they wire together.

– John Assaraf[7]

By recalibrating the way you think, you will recalibrate what you do. As we recalibrate our thinking about fear, we overcome it. Please consider fear of a challenging conversation as an opportunity to utilize what is generally known as habituation.[51]

> Habituation refers to the fact that nervous system arousal decreases on repeated exposure to the same stimulus. In layman's terms, it means that familiar things get boring. This mechanism is

hard-wired into the human genetic program. It has clear adaptive value, because habituation to familiar stimuli allows more energy to be directed to novel stimuli, hence improving the odds of survival.

Exposure works better than avoidance on the physiological level by bringing about nervous system habituation, which is the physiological antidote to anxiety. Furthermore, it works better on three additional levels as well: physiological, behavioural, and emotional.

1. On the **physiological** level, confronting your fear instead of backing down brings about a sense of accomplishment and empowerment. Every time you confront your fear, you gain power while your anxiety losses strength ("I can tolerate it; it's difficult but not impossible; it's not the end of the world"). Every time you confront your fear you accumulate evidence of your ability to cope ("I did it yesterday, I can do it again today").
2. On the **behavioural** level, confronting your fear repeatedly helps develop skills and mastery. Mastery decreases the chance of failure, and therefore reduces the need to worry.
3. On the **emotional** level, it turns out that many anxiety problems are at their core a fear of fear. Most people who fear crowds, elevators, or planes know that these objects are not dangerous. What they fear are the sensations of fear itself. Exposure to the sensations of fear allows them to habituate to these sensations, while at the same time improving their emotional literacy, since staying in the terrain helps to learn how to navigate, manage, and work it.

Exposure isn't easy. However, living in the prison of avoidance isn't easy either, and it isn't much of a life. The short-term discomfort of exposure is the price we must pay to purchase a valuable long-term asset: a life free from debilitating anxiety.

Fear and love: Mutually exclusive

Perfect love casts out fear. (1 John 4:18)

Catastrophic expectations arise regularly from an orientation and mental set of fear. A catastrophic expectation is the belief or expectation that something awful is about to happen. Sometimes a small difficulty arises in your mind and you immediately blow it up into the beginning of something terrible. For example, you may have a persistent pain in your body and begin to imagine it is cancer. Then you begin to wonder how advanced the cancer is. Now that this fearful thought has taken root, the catastrophic expectation grows, just like cancer. Soon you become convinced that no treatment will be helpful now. It must be time to write your will.

When catastrophic expectations are activated, even if the event hasn't taken place (and most likely never will), you may have a full-blown panic attack thinking about the possibilities. Unfortunately, these possibilities dictate your choices and actions. All kinds of relationships can shut down in your life. The more you hold on to negative expectations, the more you believe in them, and the worse the fear becomes. It prevents your thinking clearly and hinders your ability to find creative solutions, in the event the catastrophe you're expecting, or something like it, actually takes place.

Realize that it is not the actual event that is causing most of the fear you are feeling, but the expectations and fantasies you are dreaming up about it. In this very moment, you can handle whatever is going on. This very moment you are safe, this very moment holds endless possibilities, and this very moment can be filled with joy.

It's the feeling Brenda Shoshanna reported in the following story in her book *Fearless: The 7 Principles of Peace of Mind*:[52]

> Suffering from a migraine, Neil Young's vision went blurry and he thought both would pass. But when symptoms persisted the next day, the Canadian music star suspected something more. He was shaving and saw something in his eye that looked like broken glass. It kept getting bigger and bigger and he knew that he had to see the doctor right away. After consulting five specialists, by the next morning the verdict was in: Young had a brain aneurism, one that required prompt attention. This was Thursday; surgery was scheduled for Monday.

Some individuals might have holed up in self-pity. Young chose to go to Nashville that very night to work on his album. The words and music came fast, some songs in less than fifteen minutes. In this state of hypersensitivity, and facing his own mortality, everything he saw inspired him. A phone message from a friend inspired the song "Falling Off the Face of the Earth." By the time he flew back to New York for surgery on March 28, 2005, Young had penned and recorded eight numbers in just four days.

Fear has a vibration that attracts certain people, events, and situations to it. When you are afraid of dogs, a dog will often sense it, bark, and maybe even attack. When you feel loving toward the animal, the dog will sense it as well, and perhaps respond in kind. There is a visceral awareness of the vibration a person emits.

Masters in the martial arts, feeling extremely secure in their ability to defend themselves, can walk down the street in a dangerous neighbourhood, and their vibrations of strength and courage can deter would-be attackers. Intuitively, unconsciously, viscerally, others sense their strength. There are also stories of Hindu *rishis* (masters) who can send out such a total and unambivalent vibration of love that wild animals will come to them and lick their hands.

Nations of the world are living in fear of terrorists, failing economies, and threats of attack. The more fear is permitted to run haywire, the worse these conditions become. As soon as we stop and begin to dismantle the fear, we will be able to get in touch with our innate peace of mind, our resourcefulness, and the solutions that are waiting to be found. There are simple solutions waiting for us, surprising solutions, and ways of turning enemies into friends. Challenging conversations are opportunities for growth, not reasons to fear.

It is of the utmost importance that we realize the urgency of the situation and firmly resolve to let go of fear and live our lives on the basis of love.

For purposes of clarity, the best definition of love, and the meaning which has the greatest relevance to the thesis of this book, is the definition which is frequently quoted around the world in marriage ceremonies:

> Love is patient, love is kind. It does not envy, it does not boast, it is not proud. It is not rude, it is not self-seeking, it is not easily angered, it keeps no record of wrongs.

> Love does not delight in evil, but rejoices with the truth. It always trusts, always hopes, always perseveres. Love never fails. And now these three remain: faith, hope and love. But the greatest of these is love.

> – Saint Paul, Corinthians 13: 4–13

So, what are the specific behaviours encompassed by the term "love" as defined within this text?

The answer is presented in the following figure:

Behaviours present and absent in the mindset of love

Behaviours Adopted	Behaviours Rejected
patient	impatient
kind	unkind
contented	envious
humble	boastful/prideful
other-seeking	self-seeking
self-control	easily angered
keeping record of right/good	keeping record of wrong/bad
rejoicing in truth	delighting in evil
trusting, hopeful, persevering	untrusting, hopeless, giving up

The truth is that love is so much stronger than fear. Even a little drop of love can dissolve and heal so much fear and pain. Yet we are often so stingy; we refuse to open our hearts and give. This stinginess, this constriction, is the effect of fear operating in our lives. Therefore, as we learn to dissolve fear we simultaneously come into the healing process of love. The practice of dissolving fear is simply the practice of love. And learning the practice of love simultaneously dissolves the fear that we feel. This is one of the most practical, urgent, and enjoyable activities to undertake.

Moments of love are happening continuously, but we do not always stop to notice them. You do not take account of them, or take them in. Take them in. Relish their effects on you. If you are preoccupied by fear, these moments of love seem unimportant. They are not unimportant! They definitely take place and deserve your attention.

Whatever you pay attention to in your life increases and intensifies

What do you want to pay attention to, love or fear? What do you want more of in your life? This is an incredibly important question. You can always choose where to focus your attention.

"Taste and see that life is good" (Psalm 34:8). This is most certainly a statement of truth. For those who live in fear, life does not taste good. But when fear dissolves, the sweetness and nourishment of life are restored.

When someone gives you a dire message, when your catastrophic expectations start to grow immediately, replace them with this statement of truth. Say to yourself, "Taste and see that life is good." Focus on that. Dwell on it deeply. When the fear has passed, you can look at whatever piece of news you were given with calmer, clearer, and wiser eyes. And if there is something that needs to be done, your innate sensitivity and intuition will reveal it to you.

Fear can be a great deceiver. When you buy into the lies it sells, it takes your time, hope, and life force from you. In exchange for the false sense of well-being fear offers, you give away your birthright.

Shoshanna goes on to illustrate with the story of Esau, who sold his birthright for a bowl of lentils (Genesis 25). Esau, the firstborn twin, was to be the heir and successor to his father and to the sacred traditions of his family. However, he preferred a happy and carefree life as a hunter and man of the fields. One day, he returned from a hunting trip exhausted and faint. His brother Jacob, feeling that Esau was unsuited to be the heir, proposed to buy the birthright from him, offering a bowl of lentils in return. Famished and caring only about his hunger, Esau willingly agreed.

Just as Esau sold his birthright for a bowl of lentils, you sell your birthright for even less. Fear takes away your true safety, goodwill, happiness, and natural power to thrive, handle difficulties, and be fulfilled. When you listen to fear's lies, obey its promptings and warnings, you've been sold a bill of goods. You've turned in the wrong direction and been robbed of time, energy, and good sense. Why would you allow this? Esau was starving for that bowl of lentils; he couldn't bear the hunger he felt. You are also starving— to feel safe and good. While you're ensconced in fear, however, it's impossible to realize what's truly good and where your real safety lies. But there is a secret beneath all this. A secret which should never be forgotten:

> Truth wipes out fear on the spot! Love and fear
> are mutually exclusive!

Even a moment of truth begins to loosen the grip of fear. All the pain, damage, and illness created by fear seem very real, but they can be dissolved quickly. As soon as you see the truth of the matter, fear loses its power to harm you. As soon as you stand in the truth and cling to it relentlessly, the healing power of love appears. It is an indisputable law of the mind.

A tremendous antidote to fear is realizing that it really doesn't mean anything. It doesn't mean you're going to get hurt, that you've done something wrong, or you're on the wrong track. It's a ghost rattling a sabre at you. It warns of things that are not taking place, stirs catastrophic expectations, and even hides true danger. In fact, fear is just a feeling based upon old thoughts, ideas, beliefs, and expectations you've been taught over and over and are trained to believe. These old thoughts and beliefs become your conditioning, which arises automatically, like heartburn when you've eaten something you can't digest.

In the Japanese tea ceremony, a distinction is made between the host and the guest. It is very important to learn how to be a host and how to be a guest. Each role is different. The host creates an environment in which to receive the guest. He welcomes the guest, is gracious and hospitable. The guest arrives, partakes of whatever the host provides, enjoys, appreciates, offers thanks, and departs. The host does not behave like a guest, nor does the guest behave like a host. If that happened, the whole world of the tea ceremony would turn upside down.

You are the host. Fear is the guest. It's important not to switch roles. When you do, your whole world turns upside down. The guest (fear) comes and goes, while you (the host) remain sitting calmly and secure, watching the passing show.

Each time fear comes, the question it is truly asking us, underneath all its bluster, is, *Can you see me for what I truly am? Will you learn to grow strong as a result of our encounter? Will you tap into the endless resources you have and see through me, or will you fold?* In a strange way, fear can be your friend, if you know how to engage it wisely.

Sounds great, but can we eliminate fear as a result of focusing on love?

How can leaders choose to think positively about challenging conversations, and so eliminate the fear that previously led to avoiding them or handling them poorly?

The necessary solution is in the habitual practice of love.

Fear as a thought choice

> *Fear is not an event, it's a thought about an event . . .*
> *The greatest fear is fear itself.*
>
> – Franklin D. Roosevelt[53]

The very first words the angel said to the shepherds announcing the coming of the Christ child were "fear not." Why? And why does fear still remain such a universal phenomenon regardless of time, place, culture?

Why do we still today succumb to the self-imposed cage of limitation we call fear?

Roosevelt's quotation presented above was the key message he presented for his 1932 inaugural speech as president of the USA. Facing the depths of the depression, FDR asserted "a firm belief that the only thing we have to fear is fear itself." It is a nameless, unreasoning, unjustified terror which paralyzes needed efforts to convert retreat into advance. A host of unemployed citizens fear the growing problem of existence. Only a foolish optimist can deny the dark realities of the moment. Yet our distress comes from a failure of substance. We are stricken by no plague of locusts. Our forefathers conquered because they believed and were not afraid. Practices of unscrupulous moneychangers know only the rules of self-seeking. They have no vision, and where there is no vision, we shall perish. This is no unsolvable problem if we face it wisely and courageously.

We are therefore obligated to find out what fear really is, to assess how we can become stronger than fear. If we overcome fear, we not only experience freedom, but we can begin to see our situation from the largest perspective possible and use our enormous inner resources that allow us to handle the most challenging of conversations. We can tap into our fundamental courage, wisdom, and creativity and let them be our guides.

Numerous writers claim that the most primal emotions are love and fear. Some will recognize that fear can paradoxically make us feel safe. They believe that fear actually protects us. At the same time, many believe that love can make us weak. This is the work of fear, creating confusion and a lack of clarity. Fear thrives on this. It destroys our basic sense of confirmation and well-being, weakens our immune system, takes us off track, and makes us prey to those who wish to control or attack us. Self-hatred is fuelled by fear. Paranoia is an extreme form of fear which can infect every aspect of our being, undermining the core of all relationships and wiping out the curiosity, openness, joy, and love that we were born with. Fear is simply "stinking thinking." Fear is essentially False Expectations Appearing Real.

Panic attacks, compulsions, obsessions, and other forms of dysfunctional behaviour can all be traced back to fear.

The other prime emotion is the key antidote to fear: the nature and power of love. It is easy to mistake infatuation, attraction, and dependency for love.

Exercises which dissolve fear allow love to arise. The positivity of love simultaneously dispenses with fear. They are two sides of the same coin. Chapter 6 spells out specific techniques based on the lessons learned while facing death at 8,000 feet at the top of Mount Ruapehu, but at this stage let us reiterate that fear truly is the enemy. The darkness of evil and the crippling of any leader's potential is fear-based. We need first to reiterate that fear is primarily a thought choice, as is leadership.

Please read at least three times, ponder, absorb, and inwardly digest the wisdom of the words of my colleague Tara Bradacs, who assisted me in writing *Five Seconds at a Time*:

> The first place we lose the battle is in our own thinking. If you think it's permanent then it's permanent. If you think you've reached your limits then you have. If you think you'll never get well then you won't. You have to change your thinking. You need to see everything that's holding you back, every obstacle, every limitation as only temporary.

Since publishing *Five Seconds at a Time*, it has become even more abundantly clear to me that my own thinking and the choice I make as to which one voice I listen to is the first and most critical determinant of my outcomes, and I will either experience success or failure (even distaste) depending upon that initial choice. "In our moments of decision the leader's destiny is determined." [pg. 63]

Fear is a devious trickster that manifests itself in numerous ways: confusion, obsession, loss of control. It can be triggered by almost anything: ideas, beliefs, memories, tastes, smells, and thoughts. You might see someone who reminds you of a cruel person in your childhood and you suddenly become flooded with fear. Or maybe you go into a meeting feeling anger, picking up on a contagious fear of others that shatters your positive mood, leaving you nervous and depressed.

Fear creeps into our minds in devious ways, such as another person threatening you, either consciously or unconsciously. You may sense that someone has perceived you negatively, and respond to their approval or disapproval with fear. Similarly, a seemingly dire message can assault you—you think that your job is threatened; your partner is flirting with someone else; the frown on your doctor's face means you have cancer. Any of these situations can give credence to an attack of fear.

Yes, *attack* is the appropriate word, because the troubling thing about the message or perceived threat is the fear it generates.

In *Fearless*, Shoshanna recommends that we realize that if you don't believe the message or messenger, fear will not appear. It is not the news you fear, but the way you react that immobilizes it.

Whenever a messenger or message triggers fear, reject it immediately. Reject it even if you are not sure whether it is true or not, because you don't have the full use of your faculties when you are in the grips of fear. Wait until the fear has faded to decide if it's true. Tell yourself that there is plenty of time to determine if the message is true. Most of the time it isn't.

Fear thrives in your belief in it. It needs you to believe the stories, ideas, positions, and fantasies that it's feeding you. It needs you to see everything it says as true, as dangerous and life threatening. Once you believe the fear, it turns your mind and heart into putty and causes paralysis.

Instead of believing in the power of fear, choose to believe in the power of truth!

Before you can see the truth of a situation and reclaim your inner freedom and the full use of who you are, you have to look fear in the eye. You must be willing to stand back and make its acquaintance. As you do, you grow to unfurl fear's misrepresentations: how it arises, what fuels it, and how it disguises itself.

The truth is that fear is a bully! The more you attribute power, strength and reality to fear, the more it takes over your life.

No matter how fast you run from fear, the more it chases you. Fear preys on those who allow it and who run away from it.

You can stop in your tracks and realize that you are simply up against a bully, and a stupid one at that. Choose to think differently.

Just stop and turn around. A bully takes its strength from your flight and your anguish. By not running away, you stop fear in its tracks. You take away its steam.

Fear makes you nervous and restless, creating the illusion that if you keep moving, stay busy, you will feel better. But any action you take that is fuelled by fear is usually destructive and ineffective. It may be extremely difficult to stop running, stand still, hold your ground, and open your eyes, but as soon as you do, things change very quickly

See yourself as unwilling to flee from the fear you are feeling. Let it know you refuse to run. Stepping back, turning around, looking the bully in the eye is all that's needed for the bully to get nervous and start to break down. It knows it is being uncovered for the unreal weakling it is. Mentally spit in fear's face!

As you do this exercise, not only are you learning how to realize your power, you are beginning to uncover, and operate from, the core of who you are.

Abandon poisonous food whenever it comes to you.

– Tibetan Proverb

Fear refuses us fulfillment. It enjoys our misery. But don't fool yourself: many of us are attached to our misery, feeling that it makes us safe and secure. If you fight your suffering, you may also be clinging on to it, refusing to let it go. Clinging to suffering is not your true wish, it is simply an effect of fear.

Every moment is a good moment. There is no better time than now to begin. *Carpe diem!*

Fear grips us by telling us we can do it later, that we have all the time in the world. We don't! We don't even know if tomorrow will come. Now is the time.

Now is good medicine for undoing fear.

> This one moment—Now—is the only thing we can never escape from, the one constant factor in your life. No matter what happens, no matter how much your life changes, one thing is certain, it is always Now. Since there is no escape from the Now, why not welcome it, become friendly with it?
>
> – Eckhart Tolle[117]

There is always some action you can take, however small, from which you can learn and grow more confidence. See what needs to be done at the moment and do it now. Take a tiny step toward a larger goal—even five seconds at a time. When you do what has to be done now, fear fades.

- Fear is the trickster underlying challenging conversations that fail.
- Fear is the trickster which generates the alarming data reported in Chapter 1, that 97 percent of business leaders fail to deal with challenging conversations.

Chapter 5

The Neuroscience of Fear

The increasingly respected and now popular field of neuroscience is the study of the human nervous system. The division now called "brain science" is most relevant to the topic of challenging conversations. The recent findings from this field add traction and hard empirical data to the validity and practicality of the argument that we become what we think, and that leadership is primarily a thought choice, not a title; a disposition, not a position.

There are two types of reasoning: hot and cold. An example of what eminent writers in the field, such as Pillay, call "cold reasoning" is a straight-forward mathematical operation of a column of numbers. Cold reasoning activates short-term memory centres only, without networking regions involved in "hot reasoning."

As soon as there is an emotional state, and that is most certainly the nature of a challenging conversation, these regions of the brain become fired:

- The prefrontal cortex (PFC)
- The anterior cingulate cortex (ACC)
- The amygdala

Activation of these brain regions is critical and invariably present when we are faced with a challenging conversation.

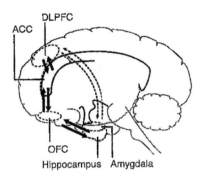

*Locations and connections between prefrontal cortex (PFC)
and the anterior cingulate cortex (ACC) and amygdala*

Of special significance to this book is the amygdala, the fear
and anxiety centre of the brain. It is important to note that it is
neurologically connected to both the PFC and the ACC.

The PFC has been shown to be the short-term memory store.
New information coming into the brain is registered here and
stored before it can be sent to long-term memory

The neuroscience of positive thought choice

Within the field of psychology, positive psychology focuses on the
energizing effects of the positive aspects of thinking and feeling.
Rather than a problem-solving approach, positive psychology
focuses on, and demonstrates the virtues as well as benefits of, a
strengths-based approach. I believe my own self-disciplined focus
and choice to hang on to the vision and expectation to see the
rising sun during my harrowing night on the mountain saved my
life. It is this positive thought choice that is the underpinning of
successfully resolving challenging conversations.

Studies have shown that leaders who have a positive outlook
on life (who display hope and gratitude) are most sensitive to

social responsibility,[54] and more specifically to greater leadership effectiveness.[55]

Positive thought choice improves the brain's ability to learn. Learning requires listening, information retention, consolidation of information packaging, and transfer to long-term-memory storage of information, and also retrieval of information. Positive thought choice and resultant positive feeling states clearly embrace learning at all these stages.[56]

Leaders may sometimes feel that positive thought choice prevents the venting of frustrations. When negative feelings such as anger do arise (and they will—we're all human, after all) understand your anger as information for a minute. This is much more effective than first telling yourself or someone else to stop being angry just because you need to be positive. Positive thought choice is not just cheerleading in the face of adversity, it's being solution-focused rather than problem-focused. When angry, ask yourself, "What do my feelings tell me?" and you'll avoid the debilitating effects of anger.

Leaders need to understand the enormously positive effects and benefits in choosing hope, happiness, optimism, mindfulness, and especially compassion. The following section of the book will enable leaders to internalize the Five Seconds at a Time techniques initially presented in my previous text.

Be warned, however, that once you begin to let go of the frustration inherent within a challenging conversation and choose to focus on a solution, the initial stages may prove the most difficult. Positive thought choice will allow you to continue your process to resolution despite the initial rough paths on your journey to the goal.

The goal is not to be perfect by the end.

The goal is to be better one second at a time.

The human brain is wired to protect us from danger. As a result, negative constraints such as fear and anxiety receive high priority for processing in the brain.

*Both consciously and unconsciously, the human
brain is geared to be in a vigilant state, and the
result of the state on thinking is profound.*

– Dr. Srini Pillay[48]

Fears that are particularly relevant to leaders include:

• Fear of failure
• Fear of layoffs
• Fear of recession
• Fear of rejection
• Fear of success

Yes, even fear of success! For example, "If I succeed, how can
I maintain it? How can I stay on top? Everyone will expect more
of me. I can't stand the pressure."

Thomas Walton, renowned for being the leading lecturer at
IBM, is reported to have said: "The fastest way to succeed is to
double your failure rate."[57]

This seems counterintuitive to being successful in dealing with
difficult conversations, but leaders must think of the discomfort
zone as a gift, as a blessing, a driving force and energy which, when
thought of as a requirement and fuel for dealing with conflict, can
transform our thinking into positive and constructive steps to the
successful resolution of differences.

The following series of brain science experiments elucidate how
fear registers in the brain and why it is so important for leaders to
understand and utilize the conscious as well as unconscious effects
of fear on the brain.

Case 1: When fearful faces were presented to subjects lying inside
an MRI scanner, the amygdala immediately lit up.[58]

When fear is the dominant emotion on our mind, it taxes our unconscious brain, which does most of the fast processing of information. This eats up valuable brain resources that could otherwise be used to resolve a challenging conversation issue.

For example: Peter, the employee mentioned earlier, confronted his boss with what he thought was unprofessional and even unethical bullying behaviour. The confrontation proved unsuccessful, resulting in Peter being fired. Understandably angry, he read up on this topic and discovered that most attempts at resolving challenging conversations fail, leading to marriage breakdowns as well as professional failures. He put this aside, but every time he came across these statistics or witnessed other challenging conversations backfiring, he became ever more fearful. His amygdala would have activated, making him even more fearful. As a result, his unconscious fear flywheel would be spinning even when thinking about something else.

This became the first level of understanding the neuroscience of the brain that was established. But even more impressive and astounding . . .

Case 2: Fear can be unconscious. What if we are surrounded by bad news, dread, and catastrophic predictions, and we're not even focusing on this negativity? Can it affect our thinking and therefore our behaviour?

The experiments which addressed this question involved what scientists call *back-masking.*

Back-masking is a procedure whereby images of emotions are presented to subjects as they are in an MRI scanner, but are flashed too quickly to be perceived by the conscious mind (for 10–30 milliseconds). Another image is presented shortly thereafter for long enough to allow people to know they can see it. It has been proven that the human brain needs an image to last longer than 30 milliseconds for the conscious brain to pick it up. We need at least that amount of time for the conscious mind to make an imprint, but the unconscious mind is still a key factor here. Experiments have found that when fearful facial expressions were shown but subjects did not know they had seen them, the amygdala still activated. That is, the amygdala picked up the fear signal unconsciously without the conscious mind knowing anything about it.

Thus, when you surround yourself with fear talk, even if you are not consciously listening to it (the news, negative workmates, minute-to-minute stock-market updater), your amygdala is still on overdrive.

In Peter's case there was a cumulative effect of the unconscious flywheel spinning. His wife became progressively annoyed at his not finding another job, and would tell him how annoyed she was. Even when he tried to tune her out and not pay attention to her, his amygdala would have picked up on this negativity. He would get his kids ready for school with the TV on, with news of bailouts, crashes, the recession, and terrorist attacks. As long as the negative information had between 10 and 30 milliseconds to register in his brain, it would dominate his unconscious emotional processor. The conclusion is that the emotional brain is endowed with a super-sensitive fear detector. The implication is that if you intuitively sense that something is wrong, don't discard this feeling just because you can't identify exactly what it is.

What can Peter do about this? Should he ignore his wife's anger and turn the news off? No, but he can deliberately expose himself to optimistic and positive influences, and thus enable his thinking brain to seek solutions without the earthquake of the amygdala. Fear creates amygdala earthquakes; positive emotions calm down the tremors and allow for decisions to be made more effectively.

Furthermore, studies have shown that when we attend to pain, the subjective experience of that pain is greater than when we do not attend to the pain. For example, subjects received a fixed amount of pain under two conditions. In the first condition, subjects rated the pain, while in the other they performed a distracting arithmetic task.

This experiment showed that not focusing on the pain resulted in lower pain ratings but higher ACC activation, thus demonstrating that an internal conflict, between focusing on the pain versus focusing on the arithmetic task, activated the ACC.

Thus, focusing on neutral or positive things rather than on the negative decreases discomfort and improves thinking. The important point here is not to focus *on* the pain, but *away* from the pain.

Why should leaders be optimistic?

Several of my clients roll their eyes when they hear the word "optimistic." In this economy, with the difficulties of balancing home and work life, with a bully of a boss . . . just the idea of optimism seems tiring to most.

With neuroscience we can adopt a radically different view of optimism and better understand what Napoleon meant when he defined a leader as "a dealer in hope."

Optimism is not the result of success, it's the cause

Hope and optimism are not "soft skills." They are necessary "hard skills" involving brain adjustments to allow your brain to navigate the path towards successful resolution of differences.

– Dr. Srini Pillay

This was demonstrated by researcher Debbie Morton,[59] who reported from her neuroscience laboratory that: "Expected positive events serve as an adaptive function by modifying behaviour in the present toward a future goal. Simulating negative events interfere with problem solving behaviour by generating negative effects of anxiety and fear."

It is important for anyone facing a challenging conversation to understand that having a positive expectation for the outcome of the confrontation helps the brain prepare to focus on its goals by capturing its attention more than fear. Future positive events are actually more impactful than past positive events on the ACC and the amygdala. That is, they replace the fear that holds the amygdala captive.

Optimism in the brain is permission to focus on a goal

Here, then, are a number of optimistic questions a leader would be wise to open a challenging conversation with to enhance goal directedness and increase ACC and amygdala activity away from fear:

- Where do you want to end up?
- What will we both get by having what we want?
- What gains will we make?
- Where can we picture ourselves when this works out?

Practical implications evolving from brain science relevant to resolving challenging conversations

1. Leaders can open a conversation by examining the past, but the brain should be left imagining positive future outcomes. In other words, never end a conversation with uncertainty.
2. Revisit the expected positive outcomes throughout the exchange.
3. When you are in conflict with someone, don't merely visit pros and cons. The more productive approach is to ask each other how things would look if you both got

your way in a manner that serves the company goals. Then work backwards from the optimistic point of having solved the problem.

4. Hope and optimism are critical tools that we can use to rewire our brains. Remember, this is not just wild speculation or cheerleading. It is instead a reframing and focus on goals, and a non-anxiety provoking vision of the future.

There are some leaders who will argue that it is not realistic to be optimistic. However, the argument evolving from brain research clearly points to findings that optimism builds the brain's connections differently than realism, and provides relief from a burning red-hot amygdala.

When you have hope and optimism, you have an automatic way of replacing fear. Hope and optimism actually open up the brain for less fear-driven processing. As a result, it is not a "soft" attitude; it actually impacts your brain and enables searches for solutions.

Summary

Many writers support the notion that attitude isn't everything, it's the *only* thing, and that our thinking is the prime factor that is within our control when dealing with challenging conversations. This necessitates the courage to step out of the comfort zone and mentally face up to the profound choice between more of the same or more of the new. Physiologically, this involves sending blood to the thinking centre rather than the anxiety centre of the brain. Neuroscientists such as Siegel, Doidge, Taylor, and Pillay all emphasize the interface between mind, brain, and interpersonal relationships between people. In particular, Pillay's CIRCA model enables us to be aware of the mental processes without being swept away by them; it helps us get off the autopilot of ingrained habitual responses and moves us beyond the emotional blocks that we all have a tendency to be trapped within.

Fear is the primary reason why people will tend to avoid or mishandle challenging conversations.

Pillay has published five steps to enable us to deactivate the anxiety centre, or amygdala, and activate the thinking centre of the brain, the prefrontal cortex. He has proven the effectiveness of the CIRCA approach to overcoming fear and thus handling challenging conversations successfully.

While fear is recognized as sometimes valuable—as when being chased by an angry bear—it must also be seen as a bully and primarily a thought choice.

The good news is that fear and love are mutually exclusive, and that love and caring is the key way to remove fear from facing a challenging conversation successfully.

Furthermore, we should realize that it's not the actual confrontation that causes the fear we feel, but the expectations and fantasies we dream up about them.

Whatever we pay attention to increases and intensifies. If we focus on the truth, then taste and see that the world is good, the grip of fear loosens. How can we choose to think positively about challenging conversations? The answer is in the habitual practice of love and caring. Fear is essentially false expectations appearing real, or, more bluntly put: stinking thinking! Optimism is not the result of success. It's the cause.

Points to Ponder

1. List your top 10 fears. Be honest. Now prioritize them.
2. Take the top three and apply each step Pillay presents within the CIRCA approach. Note the effects of this reframing.
3. Also apply CIRCA to the challenging conversation situations you recorded at the close of Chapter 2.

4. For each of the above situations, draw up a page with two columns named "optimistic outcomes" and "pessimistic outcomes." Record at least three entries in each column, and then choose to focus on the optimistic column and breathe it in. You may even choose to cut out the pessimistic column and throw it into the garbage!

SECTION B: BEHAVIOUR

Knowledge without practice is useless. Practice without knowledge is dangerous.

– Confucius

Faith without works is dead.

– James 2:14

Section B places emphasis upon the following specific behaviours which take the reader beyond content presented within the previous chapters:

- Mastery: The Art of Correction
- Dropping Judgment
- Listening First to Understand

Chapter 6

Mastery: The Art of Correction

The greatest gift you can give yourself is not only the wisest business investment you can make, but the most important aspect of dealing with challenging conversations. Without it, other strategies and approaches, no matter how brilliant or time-based, are doomed to fail.

What is this near-priceless gift?

It is your own personal development—investing in your own constant improvement (remember *kaizen*?) and betterment.

Abraham Lincoln is claimed to have said, "Give me six hours to chop down a tree, and I will spend four hours sharpening the axe."

This obviously leaves only two hours to do the actual job of chopping. That is, you should spend twice as much time working on the tools of the job as on the task itself. Spend twice as much time preparing—especially mentally—for the challenging conversation than on the actual conversation.

In a challenging conversation, what are the tools of the task? They are, simply put, *you*. You are the axe. No one knew better than Lincoln himself, who poured enormous effort and mental preparation into making himself the strongest, sharpest, truest axe and US president he could be.

The history books inform us that Abraham Lincoln was a remarkable example of persistence and self-improvement. Born into poverty, Lincoln faced defeat throughout his life. He could have quit many times but he didn't, because he adopted the mental set that saw defeat not as a reason to give up, but an opportunity to make course corrections and learn from the feedback that each experience offered him. This mental set was what resulted in his becoming one of the greatest presidents in the history of the United States of America. Here is a sketch of his self-improvement path to the White House:

1816: His family was forced out of their home. He had to work to support them.

1818: His mother died.

1831: Failed in business.

1832: Ran for state legislature—lost.

1832: Also lost his job—wanted to go to law school but couldn't get in.

1833: Borrowed some money from a friend to begin a business, and by the end of the year he was bankrupt and spent the next seventeen years paying off this debt.

1834: Ran for legislature again—won.

1835: Was engaged to be married—his sweetheart died and his heart was broken.

1836: Had a total nervous breakdown and was in bed for six months.

1838: Sought to become speaker of the state legislature—defeated.

1840: Sought to become elector—defeated.

1843: Ran for Congress—lost.

1846: Ran for Congress again—this time, won. Went to Washington and did a good job.

1848: Ran for Senate of the United States—lost.

1849: Sought the job of land officer in his home state—rejected.

1854: Ran for Senate of the United States—lost.

1856: Sought the vice-presidential nomination at his party's national convention—got less than 100 votes

1858: Ran for US Senate again—again he lost.

1860: Elected president of the United States.

Abraham Lincoln's remarkable track record of self-improvement was what prompted him to state that, "Your own thought choice and resolution to succeed is more important than anything else."

It was also his mental state that made him famous for saying, "When you reach the end of your rope, tie a knot and hang on."

This could well be reworded as follows:

> When you reach the end of your rope with another person and you need another challenging conversation, pause, prepare, focus on positive desired outcomes, and then care enough to confront.

Back to Lincoln's analogy of the tree and axe . . .

My data suggest that 49 percent avoid it, and of the remaining 51 percent, 48 percent, when faced with a tree in their way, grab that axe—dull or not—and begin whaling away at it, hacking aggressively. If the tree proves resistant, they quit, probably complaining and muttering something about it being the tree's fault or inherent nature.

So it is with challenging conversations.

Forty-nine percent avoid. And the 48 percent of those who attack the situation (i.e., the other person) do so with aggression and probably built-up anger. The person who attacks another person is probably motivated by the desire to be brutally honest. It is argued, however, that there is no place for brutality in any relationship, professional or personal. Steve's example illustrates that the 48 percent of people who *do* confront do so from a position of wanting to get even or to have it out once and for all, or they simply choose to be brutally honest. Steve inwardly fumed at his boss, Peter, who yet again used sarcasm and publicly put him down in front of his peers during a department meeting. Steve did two short-term things:

1. Avoided Peter for the rest of the afternoon. Even when Peter was observed heading for Steve's office, Steve pretended to be on the phone and simply brushed Peter off with, "Sorry, Pete. I'll come see you before I go home." He didn't.
2. Went home early and complained bitterly to his wife, Janet, who expressed her anger at Steve for dumping on her, and demanded that Steve go confront Peter and "have it out with him, once and for all."

This is exactly what Steve did, once and for all. He lost his job.

Obviously, the anger and decision to be brutally honest with Paul lacked the necessary and appropriate mental set.

Steve confused being brutally honest with successful conflict resolution—where both sides are mutually satisfied with the final outcome.

How you swing the axe, in what arc, where precisely you hit the trunk, the rhythm of your strokes—these are all techniques, skills, and tactics which can be observed, measured, evaluated, and improved. But it all begins with the axe . . . and the axe is you.

Continuous improvement, the Japanese *kaizen*, is a fundamental necessity to mastery. It lets you choose the mental set required to move yourself into the alarmingly small percentage (3 percent) of those who handle challenging conversations with the required grace and sharpening of the axe. In *Seven Habits of Highly Effective People*,[60] Stephen Covey uses the phrase "sharpen the saw." He uses a different tool but acknowledges the same requirement of continued improvement and preparation for the challenging conversations that will come your way, whether you like it or not.

Jeff Olson[61] similarly points to the crucial importance of constant improvement. He also contributes to explaining the findings that a mere 3 percent of business people successfully resolve challenging conversations. He points to the alarming statistic that out of the millions of high school graduates across North America, 58 percent—more than half—never read a book again *for the rest of their lives.*

Reading, of course, is but one relatively small way to implement *kaizen*, but it serves to illustrate the key necessity to adopt and establish a mental set committed to constant improvement. The question is: Are you developing yourself? Are you building your dream, or only your boss's?

At the beginning of my MBA course entitled "Leadership . . . a Habit of Mind," I enjoy asking the students the following question, taken from the work of Feldman and Spratt:[62]

Five frogs are sitting on a log.
Two decide to jump off.
How many are left on the log?

If you answered three, your mathematical skills are fine. But this is not a math question, it's a challenging-conversation question, and, in fact, a *life* question. The correct answer is five, because two of the frogs only *decided* to jump. There is a subtle but profound difference between *deciding* and *doing.*

Yes, thought choice is crucial, but it's only half the picture. Life is not a spectator sport, it's a contact sport. There are no practice sessions, and you've been in the game since day one, since birth. Life exists in the here and now. That's why Ralph Waldo Emerson, a noted philosopher and essayist, stated, "Do the thing, and you shall have the power."[63]

It is worthy of special note to realize that this is not a reversible strategy. Please note: you don't get the power and then go to do the thing. Many try to do it that way and spend their lives gathering the power and doing nothing. The only way to have the power is do the thing. Nike is right: *just do it.* The 49 percent of business leaders who avoid challenging conversations are probably still focusing on trying to get the power.

There is both truth and wisdom in the old Chinese proverb that your high school teacher probably urged you to remember: "The journey of a thousand miles begins with the first step."

Just do it. Learn by doing. Fire the rocket off! If you're not doing, you're dying.

To say I read scripture every day would be a lie. Some days I miss studying what I firmly believe are God-inspired words. But I can desire honestly to read it regularly on most days of my life.

An interesting thing happened last Tuesday. The system I am adopting to study the Bible is designed to enable the reader to cover the whole sixty-six chapters in one year, and when I was reading Proverbs 27, I discovered that less than a year ago I had underlined the passage: "As a man thinketh, so is he" (v3).

What surprised me was that I immediately underlined it again, because it was extremely pertinent to the book I was working on, this very one. Yet, I had not remembered previously underlining it. This actually happens to me frequently; I am constantly discovering and rediscovering insights in books that I have already read before. Why? Not simply because my memory is failing, but because of the constant changes and learnings I have experienced in the interim. My experiences change my perspective. Now, when I read what I'd read before, I understood it in a way I could not have understood it a year ago. That in turn modifies my behaviour. When I go to my activities tomorrow, I can apply my learnings from King Solomon in a way I would not have thought about a year ago, or even before last Tuesday. This reminds me of what Confucius said: "Knowledge without practice is useless."

But please note that he also stated: "Practice without knowledge is dangerous."

Learning and doing are both critical. Book smarts are not better than street smarts, or vice versa. They are both critical. One without the other is either useless, even dangerous. Thinking (thought choice) and doing becomes a never-ending cycle of continuous improvement, like climbing a ladder of challenging conversations: right foot, left foot, right foot, left foot. Try climbing a ladder with just one foot.

Not only do thinking and doing work together in a rhythm, each amplifying the other, but the truth is neither can work without the other.

This back-and-forth rhythm is extremely important and central to dealing successfully with difficult conversations. Choose a thought (a), take action (b), change your thought (c), modify your action (d), etc. This ping-pong, second-by-second process is the underpinning to dealing successfully with challenging conversations. You move back and forth constantly, making minute corrections to the course you are on, depending on the feedback the other person offers you.

The shortest path between two points is a straight line, right? Wrong. While it may be true in theory, it is not true in reality. In the real universe, everything is curved. We live in reality, not in theory. Even when you are driving along what appears to be a dead-straight road, check your hands on the steering wheel. They move the steering wheel with minute and constant corrections. These second-by-second corrections are so familiar to us we tend to overlook their significance. If you were to hold the wheel tightly in place, you'd be off the road in less than a minute. Challenging conversations are like that. Constant correction is required, regardless of how much preparation, will power, and resolve you have toward the other. In preparing and sharpening your axe for a challenging conversation, please remember to predict the unpredictable balance of thought, choice, and doing. Always predict that there will always be something unpredictable.

The following analogy still gives me goosebumps when I think of its implications and applications to challenging conversations. The following two questions form the basis for this profound analogy.

Who made history on the date July 20, 1969?

Most readers will likely know the correct answer is Neil Armstrong, when he was the first person ever to walk on the moon. His famous words "one small step for man, one giant leap for mankind" represent that the fulfillment of the vision to land on the moon, initially stated by President J. F. Kennedy, was realized.

Here is a pictorial representation of the journey made by this history-making rocket:

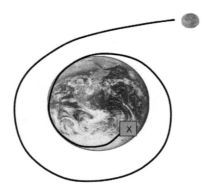

Now here is the second question:

What was the percentage of time that the history-making rocket was precisely on track?

The answer, which NASA has published, is a mere 3 percent. That is, 97 percent of the time the rocket was off track and in need of correcting. Had the people back on Earth not been constantly monitoring the rocket's progress while it was travelling in outer space, it would not have made the history-making achievement.

What the path of the rocket was *really* following is portrayed by the wiggly line here:

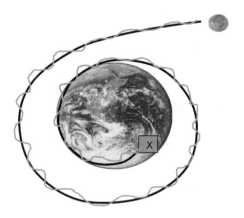

The computers constantly monitoring the progress of the rocket play an absolutely crucial role in enabling great accomplishment. Conclusion: Mastery is the art of correction, not protection.

This analogy screams out its relevance to human problem solving, including dealing with challenging conversations. Unless we have flexibility and adaptability by constantly reading and responding to feedback presented by another person with whom we are having a challenging conversation, we will not be successful.

No matter how much preparation you put into planning a challenging conversation with someone, you will be unable to predict every second of the interaction. You absolutely must listen, accept the other's response, and correct in the light of the feedback. The humbling reality is that no one is perfect, and even the most intelligent and sincere person is likely to be off track during a challenging conversation. Yes, 97 percent of the time. That's life.

The future depends not upon the super-strong.
The future belongs not upon the super-intelligent.
The future belongs to the super-adaptable.

Similarly, successfully dealing with people with whom we have challenging conversations depends upon our constant correction, one second at a time.

While I once dealt with the horrendous challenge of staying alive during the longest night of my life, five seconds at a time, I now realize that I need to be even more aware and reflective, second by second. Five seconds is actually a long time to make accurate and appropriate decisions. I can easily mess up within five seconds. What is required of me to be really successful in challenging conversations is to be open to correction second by second, one second at a time!

The goal is not to be perfect by the end. The goal is to be better one second at a time.

That was the beacon for Jamie Clarke, who was the first Canadian to climb Mount Everest, which he did on May 23, 1997. The connection with the moon landing and his success was that it was his *third* attempt. He regarded each previous attempt not as a failure, but as an opportunity to learn from each experience and correct his "rocket" to the roof of the world. After each of the attempts prior to the success of 1997, he asked the crucial questions: "What have we learned, and what corrections will we make?" His attitude of constant correction and application of *kaizen* principles led to his ultimate success. Jamie Clarke regarded the first two failures as guiding posts, not hitching posts.

Which mental set do you adopt?

In a video entitled "Your Summit Awaits," Clarke pointed out that the team's first attempt failed primarily because they failed to deal with challenging conversations. He eloquently uses running out of toilet paper as an example of avoiding bigger issues. The team began to complain and focus on the relatively minor issue of their supply of toilet paper running out rather than talk openly about major issues of possible frostbite, avalanches, failure, or even death.

> We focused on toilet paper like it was some kind of big deal. Inconvenienced, sure, but it's just toilet paper. The real problem was we weren't being honest. We weren't being honest with ourselves or the situation. Friendships were being damaged. Not being honest, we fought about toilet paper as a way to avoid the more uncomfortable, more important issues. And, in the end, nothing was resolved. Because of this avoidance, our expedition lost its best chance to reach the summit.

It was only when Clarke faced previously avoided challenging conversations and adopted a different mental set toward them that he successfully made history as the first Canadian to summit Everest. The radical thought-choice change involved adopting a mental set of previously so-called "failures" as opportunities for correction. His success was the result of adopting the same philosophy as Thomas Watson, IBM's founding CEO, did when he stated:

> Would you like the formula for success? It's quite simple really. Double your rate of failure. You're thinking of failure as the enemy of success. It isn't at all. You have a choice . . . you can be discouraged by failure, or learn and improve from it. So go ahead and make mistakes, make

all you can! You'll find success on the other side
of failure.[64]

A summary of the crucial importance of mental set and action
and the internal gyroscope of constant correction being possible
was beautifully stated by John MacDonald when he said, "You
return again and again to the proper course—guided by what? By
the chosen thought and picture of the place you are headed for."[65]

To deal successfully with challenging conversations, his words
of wisdom could be paraphrased as follows:

> Because you're off track when handling
> challenging conversations 97 percent of the
> time, you make a thought choice of anticipated
> success and constantly correct in the light of the
> feedback the other person is giving you, verbally
> or non-verbally.

The expression "it's not how you plan your work, it's how
you work your plan" falls short of what is really required in a
challenging conversation. Both how you plan your work (sharpen
your axe) and how you work your plan (correct your rocket) are
required to get you into the top 3 percent of the people in the
world who successfully handle challenging conversations.

Summary

Chapter 6 argues that investing in your own personal development,
betterment, or *kaizen*, is the underpinning to the successful
handling of life's challenges, including challenging conversations.
Abraham Lincoln is cited as a remarkable example of persistence
and self-improvement. Born into poverty, Lincoln faced defeat
throughout his life. Before becoming an eminent president of the
United States, he could have quit many times, but he didn't. He

adopted the mental set that saw defeat not as a reason to give up, but an opportunity to make course corrections. It was his positive attitude that prompted his famous saying: "When you reach the end of your rope, tie a knot and hang on." This could well be reworded as: "When you reach the end of your rope with another person and you need another challenging conversation, pause, prepare, and focus on positive desired outcomes and then care enough to confront."

This chapter has presented three interrelated points as the underpinnings to successfully handling challenging conversations:

1. The analogy of the history-making rocket to the moon has been used to show the absolute need constantly to correct. Mastery within challenging conversations is the art of correction, not protection (that is, choosing to be blind to ourselves or others). The humbling truth is that 97 percent of the time we are at least a little off track and thus need the flexibility and adaptability repeatedly to correct and modify our originally anticipated moves. This implies the necessity to expect the unexpected throughout any challenging conversation. The future belongs not to the super-strong nor to the super-intelligent, but to the super-adaptable.

2. The technique previously named "Five Seconds at a Time" has proven insufficient to ensure a successful resolution of challenging conversations. We can too easily mess up out decision-making process in less than five seconds. There is a need, therefore, to refine the technique to "One Second at a Time."

3. The success of Jamie Clarke's climb to the top of Mount Everest (May 23, 1997—very close to my near-death experience at Mount Ruapehu) was attributed to his overcoming the temptation to avoid challenging conversations. During previous attempts to reach the peak,

the team had fought over the depletion of toilet paper as a way of avoiding the more uncomfortable issue of possible injury or death. In the end, nothing was resolved, and the expedition lost its chance to reach the summit.

Jamie also discovered that Mount Everest represented more than the world's highest pile of rocks and snow. It represented the necessity to come to grips with fear in a much bigger challenge.

> Standing on the ladder, I began to understand what we were trying to conquer. For years I thought it was rock, snow, wind, and gravity. How wrong I was. A climber's biggest challenge is fear. But fear isn't the enemy of only climbers.
>
> – Jamie Clarke[66]

Fear is the main reason 97 percent of challenging conversations are avoided or fail. We need, therefore, to look closely at what fear really is: stinking thinking! Mastery is the art of correction, not protection.

Points to Ponder

1. Recall an easily remembered and challenging conversation which failed miserably. Identity the points during the exchange where you were even slightly off track.
2. Rewrite the script by answering the question: "If I did it again, what would I do differently?"
3. If possible, go back to the person and actually implement while maintaining a flexible readiness to modify on the spot, or role play with a trusted friend. Ask them to take on the role of the person with whom you previously failed to communicate satisfactorily.

Chapter 7

Dropping Judgment

Judging others makes us blind, whereas love is illuminating.

– Dietrich Bonhoeffer[67]

Bonhoeffer, a greatly respected philosopher and theologian of the last century, went on to elaborate by stating that by judging others we blind ourselves to our own evil and to the graces which others are just as entitled to as we are.

The Bible also warns us not to judge: "Do not judge, or you too will be judged. For in the same way you judge others you will be judged, and with the measure you use it will be measured to you" Matthew 7:1.

Yet we all know just how easy it is to judge another too quickly, even if we don't verbalize it. Why is that?

Firstly, it is central to handling challenging conversations successfully that we distinguish between judging others and being judgmental.

We have to judge in order to live… to know what is safe or dangerous, good or bad, healthy or unhealthy, appropriate or inappropriate. But being judgmental implies you think of yourself as better, superior, or the only one who is right. This attitude spells death in any attempt to deal successfully with a challenging conversation, as it portrays a mental state which is based on win/lose not win/win. In a challenging conversation, when by definition emotions such as anger are high, you can guarantee that when hatred judges, the verdict is guilty.

Secondly, we cannot change another's behaviour. All we can do is offer them an environment in which they can change. The central importance of dropping judgmentalism is the fact it starts with you and me. We must be accountable and take responsibility only for our own behaviour when engaged in a challenging conversation, ironic as that may sound.

> *The way that other people judge me is none of my business.*
>
> – Denis Shackel

As fallible human beings, we often fail to balance truth with grace, honesty with love, judgment with caring. The Value Ladder is a constructive way to deal with this human tendency and avoid being brutally honest, or so loving that you repress or ignore your own point of view. The sequence of steps referred to as the Value Ladder, now published by Wiley, who distributed the Workplace DiSC® materials. The figure below presents the various rungs on the ladder and clearly has *judging* as the lowest rung.

Valuing Differences
Appreciating Differences
Respecting Differences
Understanding Differences
Judging Differences

Rungs of the Value Ladder

Most readers would probably easily recognize the necessity to climb the ladder and most certainly get off the bottom rung, even if we recognize how easy it is to fall into the judging trap.

To climb to the *understanding* rung is relatively easily accomplished by recognizing the usefulness of a tool such as the DiSC Workplace® described in Chapter 2. This behavioural profile enables us to realize that 75 percent of the world has different motivators, priorities, and stressors than we do. This understanding makes it relatively easy to climb to the rung which bears its name.

In order to advance higher still all we need to do is recognize and choose to see differences as simply different and not better or worse.

Besides, consider this:

> *The people at the bottom are the ones who get us to the top. Treat them with respect.*

> – Simon Sinek[68]

All that is needed is the thought choice to agree with this and recognize the truth, wisdom, and beauty of this axiom, and we have stepped from *understanding* to *respect* and on to *appreciating* others' differences.

So what is the difference between *appreciating* and *valuing* differences? Why is *valuing* the top rung, and thus the level most relevant to handling challenging conversations successfully?

According to the Webster's Dictionary, appreciating differences involves understanding the work or value of the other, whereas valuing differences is to give someone or something even greater esteem and to prize differences on a higher level. *Valuing* is *appreciating* + *gratitude* for differences, leading meaningfully and ultimately to honouring them..

The following bullets are axioms designed to affirm and reiterate the danger of judgmentalism and the necessity for avoiding it when dealing with a challenging conversation:

- Never be defined by your past. It was just a lesson, not a life sentence. Avoid self-judgment or condemnation.
- "Most people work hard to keep their body happy. Then they seek to stimulate the mind. Then, if there is time, they look after their soul. Yet the most beneficial priority has it just the other way round." – Neale Walsh[69]
- Stress in all its forms can slowly or suddenly take your life.
- When we're frustrated, disappointed or angry, it's difficult to dive down and speak from your soul where your real truth lies. We tend to react from the emotions of our heart and fears in our mind, and wonder why.
- A judgment-free space allows you to begin a soul-to-soul conversation.
- "We come to love not by finding a perfect person, but by learning to see an imperfect person perfectly." – Sam Keen[70]
- To speak from our heart, we need to be connected to our soul.
- Serenity is the state of being we discover when we release judgment to accept what we cannot change: how others think, act, and respond to you.
- Some of us have mastered the art of burying our feelings so much that we are not aware of what we authentically feel. Getting beneath to our vulnerable feelings means we are tapping into an underlying value that doesn't feel right.
- If you feel offended, someone is treating someone else in ways you would not dream of. That dream belongs to you. See if you can understand their choices even though they don't work for you. Then you will know *what* you disagree

with instead of thinking about *who* you disagree with, as they're being a jerk.

- If you have told yourself too many times a battle isn't worth fighting, consider that recurring unfought battles build on each other, and settle into "You just don't get me," creating tension that will eventually erupt.

- We tend to blame circumstances for our mistakes, but if someone else makes a mistake, we blame them instead.

- We tend to notice things that confirm what we already believe and ignore what does not.

- Conflict happens when we project our truth onto others based on our experiences, when it's their own experiences, ones that we don't know or understand, that gives them their unique truth.

- We tend to think of truth as absolute, where one person is telling the truth and the other is lying. It is rarely this simple, thus it is difficult to reach clear resolutions. Truth is relative to each person's experience.

Chapter 8

Listening First to Understand

The most basic and powerful way to connect to another person is to listen. Just listen. Perhaps the most important thing we ever give each other is our attention.

– Rachel Naomi Remen[71]

My sister Kathleen was visiting my family and me one Christmas, three years after we tragically lost Bruce and that phenomenally emotional conversation we experienced shortly after the helicopter picked me up off the mountain.

This was the most challenging conversation of my life, as the plan to climb was my idea, and I had approached that meeting with fear. I had up to this time avoided any conversation about what had been plaguing me for three years.

Sitting on the couch, Christmas carols playing in the background and glasses of wine in our hands, I began with a loaded question: "Kathleen, can I ask you a question about the conversation we had when we first met after Bruce's death?"

"Yes, sure."

"Do you remember the meeting just before the helicopter took me off to the hospital?"

"Of course. I'll never forget it."

"No, neither will I."

She leaned forward, touched my arm and said, "It's okay, I can talk about it. What's on your mind?"

"Do you remember your very first words to me, after we both stopped shaking uncontrollably and we'd caught our breath?"

"Hmmm, I think so. What do you remember?"

"Your very first words were, 'Thank goodness it wasn't you,' and I've been puzzled ever since by what you meant. I thought you and Bruce had a fabulous relationship, and I just don't understand why you may have loved me more."

Kathleen took several seconds before stating, "Oh, Denis! I didn't say that. What I said was, 'Thank goodness it wasn't you *too*.'"

What a radical difference!

I had avoided this challenging conversation for three years and it turned out to that my fear was self-imposed, self-created thinking and simply wrong.

Who is correct? We will never know. Did she really say the key word "too," or did I simply not hear it? Was I illustrating what Paul Simon sings as the key line in "The Boxer": *Man hears what he wants to hear and disregards the rest*?

This true story supports the necessity to identify *listening* as the fundamental underpinning to dealing successfully with challenging conversations.

Firstly, let us distinguish between *listening* and *hearing*. They are not the same.

Hearing refers to the sounds that you hear, whereas listening requires focus. Listening means paying attention not only to the story or message presented to you, but how it is told, the words chosen, the intonation of the voice and how the sender uses their body language. Listening means being aware of both verbal and non-verbal behaviour.

Your ability to listen effectively depends upon the degree to which you perceive and understand these messages.

The ground-breaking work of American psychology professor Albert Mehrabian[72] showed that the percent of meaning transmitted by each channel of communication was as follows:

- Language (words, written or spoken): 7 percent
- Intonation (the music of your voice): 38 percent
- Kinesics (body language): 55 percent

The profound implication is that effective listening must involve listening with your eyes and a gut feeling, as well as the ears.

Secondly, adults spend an average of 70 percent of their waking hours communicating. But of this, 55 percent of the time is spent listening.[73]

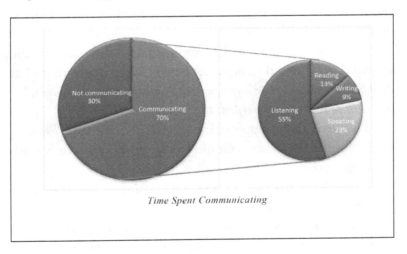

Time Spent Communicating

Thirdly, an effective listener will pay attention to what is being said, but also to what is being left unsaid or only partly said. Those who successfully negotiate challenging conversations observe language and notice any consistencies between verbal and non-verbal messages. Research clearly shows that where inconsistencies exist, the effective listener will involuntarily believe the non-verbal cues over the verbal message. Thus, if a person goes instantly red in the face and yells, "I'm not angry!" this is perceived by an effective listener as actually a lie.

The above three points are common sense and known by the reader, but overwhelming evidence[74] shows that they are not in common practice. The majority of people easily fall into the trap of listening to *reply* rather than to *understand*. This trap generates defensiveness and spells disaster for any challenging conversation. As soon as you catch yourself or hear someone else beginning a sentence with the word "but," you can bet that they are not listening to understand but listening to be understood. They are using their truly remarkable brain, which processes information in a miraculously short time, to generate a counterargument rather than seeking truly to understand the other's point of view.

The following are seven specific behaviours that facilitate effective listening during any challenging conversation:

1. *Stop talking and just listen*

As Mark Twain is reported to have said, "If we were supposed to talk more than listen, we would have two tongues and one ear."

The principle is supported by the truth and wisdom in acknowledging that well-timed silence has more elegance than speech. Ironically, music without the rests is just noise; your speech without a pause to listen is similarly just noise.

When someone else is talking, listen, do not interrupt, talk over them, or finish their sentence.

2. *Empathize*

> *Never criticize a man till you have walked a mile in his moccasins.*
>
> – Mary Torrans Lathrap[75]

Seek to understand the other's point of view. Empathy is at its simplest an awareness of the feelings and emotions of another person. It becomes a key link between self and others, because it's how we understand what others are experiencing as if we are feeling it ourselves. Empathy goes considerably further than sympathy, which is *feeling for* someone. Empathy instead is *feeling with* the other, through our imagination and thought choice.

Australian comedian Tim Minchin points out that, "Empathy is intuitive, but is also something you can work on intellectually."[76]

Empathy also involves thought choice and a mental set of commitment to keeping an open mind. Thus, we can identify three related but different types of empathy, all of which are required as underpinning to success in dealing with challenging conversations:

1. **Cognitive empathy** is "perspective taking": being able to project yourself into someone else's place, and see their perspective without necessarily engaging with their emotions. Cognitive empathy is empathy by thought rather than by feeling.

2. **Emotional empathy** is "emotional contagion," being able to feel the other's emotions alongside them as if you have "caught" the emotions.

3. **Compassionate empathy** is feeling someone's pain and taking action to help. Like empathy, compassion is about feeling concern for someone but with an additional move toward action to mitigate the problem.

In challenging conversations, a balance between these three types of empathy is required. The other person as a rule does not want or need you simply to understand (cognitive empathy), and they don't need you just to feel their pain alongside them (emotional empathy). Instead they need you to understand and sympathize with what they are going through and, crucially,

take action or help them take action to resolve the problem
(compassionate empathy).

4. Finding the balance between logic and emotion is the
   outcome of exercising compassionate, loving, empathy.
   (See Section C for guided practice in this skill.)

3. Recognize subjectivity

Everyone is essentially subjective in their perception and objectivity
is an unattainable ideal. We all look at the world, and others,
through our own unique filters as if we are looking through the
coloured panes of a stained-glass window.

> *The locus of the human mystery is perception of this*
> *world. From it proceeds every thought, every act.*
>
> – Marilynne Robinson[77]

> *Be thankful for what you have . . . you'll end up*
> *having more. If you concentrate on what you don't*
> *have, you will never ever have enough.*
>
> – Oprah Winfrey[78]

> *Everything that irritates us can lead us to an*
> *undertaking of ourselves.*
>
> – Carl Jung[79]

> *Change the way you look at things and the things*
> *you look at change.*
>
> – Wayne Dyer[80]

4. *Listen for ideas, not just words*

When in a challenging conversation, strive to grasp the whole picture, not just isolated bits and pieces. This is perhaps the most difficult listening skill; it necessitates focusing, avoiding distractions, and waiting till the speaker has finished.

Beware of selective listening which by definition drops parts of the whole picture.

5. *Strive for collaborative conversation*

Resist treating the conversation as if it is a competition. Approaching the person with a spirit of competition guarantees poor listening, because discussion becomes a contest with a score being kept for who wins the most points by arguing.

Affirming points of agreement rather than highlighting them leads to more effective listening.

A simple technique to accomplish this listening goal is to switch the beginning of a sentence from "yes, but . . ." to "yes, and . . ." and "no, but . . ." to "no, and . . ."

The fourth habit from Stephen Covey's *Seven Habits of Highly Successful People* is "think win-win."

6. *Implement active listening (paraphrasing)*

Abraham Maslow, still regarded as a world authority in human needs and motivation, stated that "the deepest need of the human soul is to be understood."[81]

The foundation of understanding is the willingness to listen, and furthermore, "most people listen in order to reply, not understand," according to Covey, and previously St Francis.

7. *"Seek first to understand before being understood"*

The last and most powerful principle and technique for effective listening during a challenging conversation is best summed up by these words of Stephen Covey's.

The mechanics and actual techniques to accomplish this goal boil down to the following four levels of truly empathic listening:

1. **Mimic the content:** Repeat what the other just said. This ensures that you are in fact listening and the other knows you are. The huge benefit of mimicking is that there is no place for judgment.
2. **Rephrase the content:** Tell the same story but in your own words. You not only show the other you are listening, but also that you understand what the other is saying.
3. **Reflect on feelings:** Focus on the emotions that lie behind what is told, not on the words that express these emotions.
4. **Rephrase the content and reflect the feeling:** This is a combination of the second and third form of empathic listening. It shows that you are really listening and understanding what message lies behind the words.

Tower of Babel

To summarize and emphasize the central importance of listening to understand, the following story illustrates the interconnectedness of listening to *speak the same language* as the person with whom you are involved in a challenging conversation.

The story known as the Tower of Babel is recorded in various traditions and portrayed by artists such as Pieter Bruegel the Elder (1563), M.C. Escher (1932), and A.M. Mallet (1719).

Breugel's Tower of Babel, Escher's Tower of Babel

Mallet's Tower of Babel

Jewish Tradition

People built the tower in order to make a name for themselves and take God's place in the heavens.

The Jewish historian Flavius Josephus in his *Antiquities of the Jews* recorded that it was Nimrod who had the tower built. Nimrod was a tyrant who tried to turn the people against God, who had previously sent the flood to cleanse the earth (story of

Noah). The tower was to be tall enough to remain above the waters, which had not taught them to be godly.

God saw the motive as disrespectful and an arrogant effrontery, so He confused their language so they could not understand each other. The word *babble* derives from this story and shows the necessity for people to "speak the same language," or remain in confusion. The foundation remains are located in Babylon.

> *And the Lord said, If as one people speaking the same language they had begun to do this, then nothing they plan to do will be impossible for them.*

> – Genesis 11:6

Islamic Tradition

The Qur'an has a similar story, although it's set in Egypt. Pharaoh asks Haman to build a stone tower so that he can mount up to heaven and confront the God of Moses.

Mormon Tradition

In the *Book of Mormon*, a man named Jared and his family ask God that their language not be confounded at the time of the Tower of Babel. Because of their prayers, God preserved their language and led them to King Nimrod in Babel, who ultimately directed them to travel across the seas to the Americas.

Surely the story, whichever tradition you prefer to believe, has a profound significance to dealing successfully with challenging conversations.

A phrased summary could well be: When people speak the same language, share understanding and value differences, nothing they plan to do will be impossible!

Summary

We are all essentially subjective in our perception of the world, including others with whom we may well have strong differences of opinion. Objectivity is essentially an unattainable ideal. In any challenging conversation we must do our utmost to be open to someone else's version of reality.

Chapter 7 acknowledges the ease with which we judge another's behaviour yet stresses how destructive that tendency is on the relationship. It must be noted, however, that it is not the act of simply judging that is problematic; it is when we fall into the judgmentalism of thinking we are better, worse, or maybe superior to the other that a challenging conversation proves potentially disastrous. These words of Bonhoeffer are featured as a fundamental truth: "Judging others makes us blind, whereas love is illuminating." Equally important is the axiom that the way others judge us is none of our business.

Chapter 8 stresses the crucial importance of listening while dealing with a challenging conversation. My personal example of dealing with my sister immediately after she discovered that she had lost her precious husband illustrates the profound necessity to seek first to understand before being understood. Did Kathleen say, "Thank goodness it wasn't you too," or did she say, "Thank goodness it wasn't you"? There is no proof of where the truth lies, although I suspect I failed to listen accurately, and as a result failed to understand what she actually said. The fear of being rejected by Kathleen most likely drove me foolishly to seek first to be understood ahead of seeking to understand. This experience also illustrates how the fear associated with meeting Kathleen drove me to avoid confronting her till three years after the event. In hindsight, how easy it is now to understand the 49 percent of the sample used in the study who chose to avoid a challenging conversation rather than confront it. And I'm supposed to be a trained expert in the field! A probable alternative could well be, "How hypocritical!" which in turn prompts me to recall the wisdom of Mark Twain who is reported to have said[110] "the best way to be successful is to follow the advice you give others."

It is only when we listen with our eyes as well as ears that we can hope to develop sufficient empathy for the other to be able to arrive at a satisfactory solution to any challenging conversation. Paraphrasing what the other said before we present our viewpoint is a simple practice to show our empathy as well as check whether we heard what was actually meant to be said. This practice also allows us to speak the same language as the other, and as the story of the Tower of Babel illustrates, the closer we can get to speaking the same language as the other, the more likely acceptable resolutions can be established. Furthermore, God's word as expressed by the writer of Genesis (probably Moses) stated that "If as one people speaking the same language they had begun to do this, then nothing they plan to do will be impossible for them."

This surely stresses the importance of the following section on practical exercises.

Points to Ponder

1. Conflict occurs when we project our own truth onto others based on our experiences, when it's their experiences that we don't know or understand that gives them their truth. The necessity to start from a caring mindset allows us to move into genuine curiosity with questions that are seeking what's going on in their world. Whatever answer comes back, receive it from a position of *just noticing*. This is the non-judgmentalism required in first seeking to understand where the other person is coming from.

Pay attention to the next several times you converse with someone.

- Are you really listening, and do you need improvement?
- Are you responding too quickly?
- Do you have to start over from the beginning?

After you evaluate your current performance level, decide where your focus will be and consider the four levels of empathic listening, and the next time you hear someone use words such as "issue," "problem," or "can you help me?" this is your cue to implement your new way of listening.

2. Re-read all the bullet points presented at the close of Chapter 7. Slowly reflect upon each one. Which rise to the highest importance for you? Now return to the personal example(s) you recorded at the close of Chapter 1. Visualize meeting with these people and apply the implications of the bullet point selected to the imaginary conversation. Take notes and record the actual conversation that led to a harmonious resolution of the issue.

   Are you going into a challenging conversation from a place of serenity that can handle whatever erupts on the other side without falling apart in despair or going into any form of attack?

3. Learn Niebuhr's Serenity Prayer by heart and then turn it into an *asking* and *listening* exercise. Preferably by yourself, and in silence, ask yourself the following:

   - What do I need to accept that I cannot change?

- What can I change for which I need courage?
- Where am I unclear about what I can and cannot change that has left me stuck?

Trust and listen deeply for answers. At first it may seem like the internal chatter of thoughts appearing, but with practice you will intuitively hear ideas and inspirations—wisdom pouring in from a place beyond your thinking mind. Record these insights as notes too.

SECTION C:
C. A. R. I. N. G.
ADOPTING A CARING MINDSET

Chapter 9

Courage to be Real

- **C**ourage to be real
- **A**pproach the challenging person with love
- **R**elease attachments
- **I**ntuition utilization
- **N**avigate to a safe harbour
- **G**enerate love

The ways we think we are, rather than the ways we truly are, are the bars on our personal prison.

– The Illuminated Rumi[82]

When King David simply said, "Taste and see that life is good" (Psalm 34:8), he stood up to fear and laughed in its face. It is a rejection of fear. It is a statement of truth. For those who love in fear, life does not taste good. When fear dissolves, the sweetness and nourishment of life are restored.

The humourist and popular film star Jim Carrey, during his address in 2014 to the graduates of Maharishi University in Iowa, stated that he attributes his success to choosing to taste and choose love over fear. He appealed to his graduating audience to do the same and take this action. He elaborated by stating:

The decisions we make in this moment . . . are based in either love or fear. So many of us choose our path on fear disguised as practicality. . . . Life doesn't happen *to* you, it happens *for* you. Sometimes, I think that's the only thing that is important. Just letting each other know we're here, reminding each other that we are part of a larger self. . . .

I used to believe that who I was ended at the edge of my skin. Slacking off has some benefits. It does allow you to separate who you truly are and what's real, from the stories that run through your head.

[The faculty] have given [the students] the ability to walk behind the mind's elaborate set decoration and see that there is a huge difference between a dog that's going to eat you in your mind and an actual dog that's going to eat you. That may sound like no big deal, but many never learn that distinction and they spend a great deal of their lives in fight or flight response . . .

Now, fear is going to be a player in your life, but you get to decide how much. You can spend your whole life imagining ghosts, worrying about the pathway to the future, but all there will ever be is what's happening here, and the decisions we make in the moment, which are all based in either love or fear. So many of us choose our paths out of fear disguised as practicality. What we really want seems impossibly out of reach and ridiculous to expect, so we never dare to ask the universe for it . . .

. . . the effect you have on others is the most valuable currency there is. . . . I did something that makes people present their best selves to me wherever I go. I am at the top of the mountain, and the only one I hadn't freed was myself and that's when my search for identity deepened.

[I've struggled with my identity, wondering] what if I showed up to the party without my Mardi Gras mask and I refused to flash my breasts for a handful of beads? . . . to find real peace, you have to let the armour go. Your need for acceptance can make you invisible in this world. Don't let anything stand in the way of the light that shines through this form. Risk being seen in all your glory. . . . [The painting "High Visibility" is] about picking up the light and daring to be seen. . . .

Our eyes are not viewers, but also projectors that are running a second story over the picture that we see in front of us all the time. Fear is writing that script and the working title is "I'll never be enough." . . . Oh, and why not take a chance on faith as well? . . . not religion, but faith. Not hope, but faith. . . . Hope is a beggar, hope walks through the fire and faith leaps over it!

You are ready and able to do beautiful things in this world . . . you will only ever have two choices: love or fear. Choose love, and don't ever let fear turn you against your playful heart.

Martin Buber, probably most famous for his classic text *I and Thou*,[83] decided that when a person is desperate and goes to another for help, what he truly needs is a presence through which he knows that, despite anguish, there is still meaning.

Buber let go of his religious practices and disregarded his name and title, all of which, he felt, had kept him from being fully present for others. Instead, he simply focused on becoming completely present and available to all of life. He focused on living from his authentic self. By discarding all the trappings and distractions, he kept himself focused on the truth of the moment. He allowed himself to have the direct experience of others and was able to respond to them from his deepest truth. When visitors came to him, they found someone at home.

He recognized that the inauthentic self is fear-ridden.

When you spend your life presenting a false front to others, it's easy to lose touch with your deepest reality—your authentic self. It becomes difficult to hear what others are truly saying or what they need from you. Your words become routine and empty; people listen and are not moved. It is only when you put aside your false self that true presence and love arise. This is the healing we all want, which brings unshakable peace of mind.

Throughout most of our lives we play a variation on the game of Let's Pretend. We say, "Let's pretend that what happened really doesn't matter. I'll help you keep your pretenses up, and you help me keep up mine." From the time we are young we are taught to create a public personality to please others and hide much that is real. Little by little, however, this false personality, or ego, takes over, and we live in constant fear of being found out—discovered to be someone other than who we seem.

Pretense robs our true life from us. If someone knocks on your door to visit, more often than not there's no one home. It can be quite scary to live in a world where it's hard to find someone really to listen, respond and care. And of course, there is nothing more healing, and no better antidote to fear and loneliness, than to find someone who is truly present with you. In those moments you become at home with yourself as well. It is little wonder then that Woody Allen is famous for saying "Showing up is 80 percent of life."

Usually we do not open our "reassurance house"; instead we spend most of our time and energy acquiring skills, knowledge, and strategies, anything to build up our false self. Unfortunately, no matter how much time and attention we devote to this, it never brings real joy or peace because it's the consequences of choosing fear over love.

No matter how much praise the ego receives, it never feels really approved of or loved. By its very nature the ego is skittish, fearful, and ungrounded. It constantly craves more and more approval, and regularly feels threatened. The ego cannot distinguish between what is useless and what is valuable. It eats too much, makes wrong choices, and refuses to face reality. Living on this basis, we live in fear. Ego is wisely perceived as Edging God Out.

According to Buddha,[84] we are all born in the grip of three poisons: greed, anger, and delusion. These poisons are afflictions, and some of us have more of one than another. They are the fuel for the ego, causing it to be defensive, suspicious, and manipulative and to camouflage itself in all kinds of ways. Yet, no matter how much powder, paint, jewels, and new clothes the ego wears, no matter how many times it hears "I love you," it basically feels ugly and hates itself and everyone else.

Let's look at an imaginary case. Even though Amy's boyfriend told her he loved her over and over again, she didn't believe him. She needed to hear it again and again. "Why do you love me?" she kept asking. Of course this became exhausting for her boyfriend, who, feeling drained, ultimately left.

Why do we cling to our disturbing egos? Because we have no idea how magnificent we truly are.

How does a false self begin to grow and gain power over us? We are born full of joy, curiosity, and the desire to grow into who we uniquely are. Each child comes into life with her own particular songs to sing, lessons to learn, challenges to face. She is able to live each moment fully, calling out for food when she's hungry, reaching for love when she feels alone. She responds to her own inner needs and callings and interacts with the world in her own particular way.

Before the demands of others take hold, before family, social, and religious conditioning kicks in, the little child has an intrinsic sense of who she is, what she can give to others, and what she needs to receive. She is a child of life, a member of the universe. There is a sense of belonging, safety, and trust that all that is needed will be provided. This is a condition of optimum well-being.

As the child grows and interacts with others, the sense she has of being at home in a safe and supportive universe fades. The world often begins to stand in opposition to her desires and can seem filled with danger. She must struggle and fight for what is hers, and suddenly has to cover up and hide. Anxiety, dread, and fear arise. Before long the child begins to feel there is something fundamentally wrong with her—that she is not loveable and doesn't belong or maybe not good enough.

Furthermore, the generally poor level of parenting and schooling which appears rampant around the world is evidenced by the research findings[85] that children by the age of only five years have been exposed to authority figures, parents, and teachers telling them *no* 285 more times than telling them *yes*. I find this disturbingly crippling to the psyche, heart, and soul of the developing child, don't you?

Here surely is another reason why 97 percent of leaders still adopt a fear-based mental set over the mutually exclusive mental set of love.

Another reminder is that a leader is "a custodian of the human spirit," as American businessman and writer Max De Pree puts it. So rather than curse the darkness of the reality that most people have been brought up in, where fear overruled love, there is surely a responsibility for today's leaders to light a candle and take a courageous step forward by countering the norm, and courageously caring sufficiently to be real. By definition this means being true to the way we were born, all as children of God "designed for success, engineered for accomplishment and endowed with the seeds of absolute greatness," according to American author Zig Ziglar.[86]

When Nelson Mandela was inaugurated as president of South Africa, this inspiring leader who had chosen love over fear, even when imprisoned for twenty-seven years, quoted Marion Williamson[87] during his now famous speech. He reminded the world that:

> Our deepest fear is not that we are inadequate. Our deepest fear is that we are powerful beyond measure. It is our light, not our darkness that most frightens us. We ask ourselves, Who am I to be brilliant, gorgeous, talented, fabulous? Actually, who are you not to be? You are a child of God. Your playing small doesn't serve the world. There's nothing enlightened about shrinking so that other people won't feel insecure around you. We are all meant to shine, as children do. We were born to make manifest the glory of God that is within us. It's not just in some of us; it's in everyone. And as we let our own light shine, we subconsciously give other people the permission to do the same. As we are liberated from our own fear, our presence automatically liberates others.

What a powerful reminder for all leaders to be real and true to their natural selves instead of caving in to the crippling, inhibiting and freezing power of fear, predictably generated by our bad habits as parents and teachers!

The poison of the Garden of Eden's serpent has taken hold. As the child leaves the natural self of childhood, she creates a self to please others, and to earn the love and approval that was originally hers. Now she is further exiled from her basic wholeness and wisdom. This split haunts many of us. Living cut off from our natural selves, there is no longer a true foundation to stand on. The whole world becomes unreal and unsafe.

> *In social moments of challenging conversations, we*
> *see how estranged we are from each other.*

> – Paul Tillich[88]

Not aware that we have rejected ourselves, we live with the constant fear of rejection by others. This fear is particularly vivid in relationships and in the workplace where there is tremendous pressure to look good, fit in, and fulfill endless demands. In order to do so, we find ourselves living more and more from the false self. Unknowingly, we have accepted the guidance of fear.

Of course, sooner or later this backfires. The resentment and despair of living as a false self is too much to bear. No one can tolerate it continually—not even Robin Williams, who shocked the world when he took his own life. It is posited[89] that this widely respected and beloved leader within the film and entertainment industry—while suffering from Parkinson's disease and an attendant neurological disorder called Lewy Body Dementia—at his core was an introvert and high "C," according to the DiSC® behavioural model, and simply could not cope with the demands of the entertainment industry to be extroverted, hilarious, and that exaggerated "i." The "C" and "i" are directly opposite. Not being true to our real self sickeningly distorts our soul. Robin was at his core a strongly introverted man who predictably was told *no* 285 times more than the affirming *yes*. Everyone needs the basic strength and resourcefulness that comes from living from and accepting the truth of who they are. Living from the false self ultimately causes panic attacks, rebellious behaviour, illness, anger, and other forms of protest. No matter what hardships come into your life, no matter what turn events take, if you have yourself you also have the natural ability to handle whatever comes along. There are tremendous gifts and inner resources available when you have the courage to be who you are.

The pressure to conform is high. Many people believe there is something wrong with them because they are different. They establish their value by comparing themselves to everyone else. But as you look at yourself through the eyes of others, you become an object to yourself and a stranger.

Here's a case study of a woman we'll call Maria:

> Maria never felt satisfied. Whatever her husband bought her was not up to par. It didn't compare with the gifts her friends received from their husbands. Her gifts weren't wrapped as well, were less expensive, and seemed to be last-minute choices. Her best friends' husbands spent considerable time, money, and attention choosing their gifts, and they received gifts more often. Little by little, this took a toll. Not only did it cause friction between Maria and her husband, but also between Maria and her friends. Instead of representing love to her, her husband's gifts began to diminish her sense of self-worth. She saw them as evidence that he didn't really care, and that she wasn't worth much in his eyes.

Maria was entirely in the grip of her false self, perched on an identity that had to fall apart. She knew her value only by comparing herself to others. She needed gifts and other outward signs of attention to affirm her identity. Her entire identity was externally based, dependent upon the behaviour and responses of others. The facts that her husband loved her dearly and that she was a worthwhile and beautiful woman were completely lost to her. What had started as a fulfilling marriage began to fall apart.

When you live from a fear-based self, you give more credence to the responses of others than to what you feel and can learn by yourself. You accept the thoughts of others as true and doubt your own feelings and responses. In this manner, you lose contact with what is authentic and meaningful and become an easy target for fear. How can you live the reality of others? Can you ever gain enough approval in someone else's eyes? Not if fear is the basis of your existence.

> *We are not leaning willows—we can and must detach ourselves. With the exercise of self-trust, new powers appear.*
>
> – Henry David Thoreau[90]

Fear warns us to conform to the reality of others or else we will be shamed and thrown away. Of course, the opposite is true. The more you extricate yourself from the reality of others and connect with and live from who you really are, the stronger, more alive, and more worthwhile your life becomes. And the less you live in the grip of fear.

So the real primary action is developing self-trust and self-love.

> *I must be myself. I cannot break myself any longer for you. I will so trust that what is deep is holy, that I will do whatever inwardly rejoices me and the heart appoints.*
>
> – Ralph Waldo Emerson[91]

From deep within all of us there is a longing to be real, to express and know ourselves fully. When you are able to take off your masks, not only can you breathe easier, but your life becomes renewed. But taking off your masks may not be so easy. You may have become so accustomed to wearing your masks that you confuse them with your own skin. Although your masks may constrict at every turn, you fight to the death to keep them on. [BTW dear reader, now you know why the cover of this book has the illustration involving the peeling off of a mask.]

Another lie that fear tells is that masks constitute your security and beauty. What's underneath is scary and ugly. Of course, this just isn't so. Some people would rather die than have their masks taken off. They cling to the masks they wear the way a shipwrecked sailor clings to a lifeboat. If the mask is insulted, they respond with fear and anger. Some would kill to uphold their public image. Some kill themselves when their image is gone. Even when they're quite ill, some people are still primarily concerned with how they look to others and the impression they will make. They live behind the fortress of their masks until the very end. But the changes we encounter in life eventually wipe out all images and take our masks and games away. Even on the death bed, many people won't talk about death, nor face what they may think of as unfinished business, especially in the form of challenging conversations with other family members.

We create masks to meet the masks of others. Then we wonder why we cannot love, and why we feel so alone. But remember, everything the mask says and does is for the purpose of hiding. Can one mask love another? Does a mask know how to communicate?

The false self becomes especially active in love relationships. For many couples, the first months of their relationship are glorious, as they live out and project their fantasies upon one another. Each becomes someone different, having left huge parts of themselves unexpressed. Naturally, this can only last so long. Usually after six to nine months, other aspects of the couple's nature begin to be revealed. This is the point when so many say, "I don't know where the love went," or, "I love you, but I'm no longer *in* love."

Of course, it is not the love that went anywhere, it is the false, fantasy self that is beginning to crack apart. The false self cannot remain indefinitely, and when other parts of our personality begin to emerge, what is thought of as love seems to disappear. Usually, we spend most of our time trying to make someone into a person who meets our dreams or needs. When he or she can't or won't change in the way we want them to, we complain that we don't know where the love went. Of course, there was no love in the first place, only need and manipulation. Here is another example:

> Charles was devastated. He idolized his mentor, the person who was everything he longed to be. After about a year of studying with him, Charles found out secrets about his mentor's life that shocked him. They were in direct opposition to everything the mentor taught and seemed to be. Charles couldn't eat, he couldn't sleep; he was struck to the core. He absolutely hated hypocrisy!

"How could he betray me like this?" Charles said over and over. "He's ruined everything. I feel like a fool for having loved him so much. Whatever he taught was garbage. I'll never trust again."

A friend of Charles listened. "You didn't love the teacher," he said. "You loved your image of him, your fantasy about who you wanted him to be. When you know the truth and still love him, then you're doing something. Otherwise, don't call it love! That's the real lesson he's teaching you."

When you build a life based upon an image of who you or another person has to be in order to be valued, you are building your life on sand—you are not really able to know or love the person, only your fantasies about them. At any moment things can change; other parts of this person can be exposed and your dreams pulled out from under you.

To experience love and connection, to become free of fear, you must be willing to accept yourself and others just as you are. You must be willing to let go of your demands that others be a certain way, or you will reject them.

Discovering your authentic self

What else is needed to live from your authentic self, to be able to dip into your innate storehouse of courage and strength? There is a wonderful Buddhist teaching from the *Laṅkāvatāra Sūtra* which helps answer this: "Don't look for what is real. Just let go of all that is unreal, and that which is real will come to you all by itself."

First you must become aware of the ways in which you cling to that which is not real: toys, fancy cars, diamonds, luxury yachts, and diversions like alcoholism, workaholism, or drug addictions. Often these provide a sense of self-worth. When you let go of that which is unreal, your authentic self will appear all by itself.

It is common for all of us to make choices that harm us: to decide to stay in deadening situations, and not to speak up about that which matters. You feel you have all the time in the world to wait for things to change. You don't. Fear tells you it is dangerous to be truthful. The real danger, however, is believing this fear and not discovering and living from your truth.

> When you have life in yourself, it is not by any known or appointed way; then you shall not discern the footsteps of any other. If we live truly, we shall see truly.
>
> – Ralph Waldo Emerson

Restoring the Self

We are constantly invited to be who we are.

– Henry David Thoreau.

Addictions and obsessions are fuelled by hunger for the true Self, and the emptiness of life without it. Once the Self is recovered, equilibrium is established and everything else falls into place.

Becoming fearless requires that you recover your authentic Self. You begin your journey to self-recovery by letting go of that which is false. Of course you can't do this until you've become aware of what is false in your life. For each of us it will be different. When one thing is let go of, another will appear. You don't have to let go of everything at once. Just peel the onion little by little until you arrive at the core, even five seconds at a time.

In order to know who you are, you must also know who you are not, what is false and unworkable in your life, and when you are living someone else's dream. You must know what feels disturbing or fundamentally out of sync with who you are: your calling, your mission, your values, your vision, and what I called "the big rocks" in *Five Seconds at a Time*. So many of us spend years of our lives twisting ourselves out of shape to conform to other people's expectations of who we are, or who we should become. Families and people who are in love are famous for projecting these images and demands upon one another. However, these expectations can be lethal. They cause pain, distortion, and lack of self-acceptance—or knowing who we truly are.

Dear reader, here is a statement of truth and medicine for curing the sick part of any leader. Pause, read, inwardly digest:

You can't say yes if you can't say no.

Fear arises because you do not choose to say no. It is not the impulsive, automatic no a child may offer out of resistance, anger, or stubbornness. It is a different kind of no. It comes from understanding and accepting who you are and who you are not. It comes from knowing what is true for you and what is false. This no is a sign of respect for yourself, recognition that it is perfectly fine to be who you are. You do not have to disguise, distort, or reject your truth. You do not have to be all things to all people.

Many of us don't know what we should say no to. We feel guilty and ashamed of not going along with everything. We feel that if we don't meet everyone's needs, we've failed or there is something wrong with us. Some leaders imagine that they should be able to belong everywhere, respond to every calling. But this scatters their energy and causes confusion. By living in this manner, you lose touch with your authentic Self and cannot develop the courage to be who you are.

If others reject you because you've said no, let them. Realize that if you can't say no, you are rejecting your authentic Self. Also, realize, that you can't say yes if you can't say no. Your yes is then not a real yes, it is an automatic, knee-jerk response. It arises out of obligation and the wish to be accepted. This is not a true yes, offered from the fullness of your being. If you can't offer a full, unconditional, unequivocal yes, then you are not living from your authentic Self. When you can say yes (or no) in an unconditional, whole-hearted manner, fear has nowhere to stick.

> *When we receive the power to say yes to life, then peace enters us and make us whole.*

> – Ralph Waldo Emerson[91]

Emerson's wisdom is affirmed by these illuminating words of William Hutchison Murray's:

Until one is committed, there is hesitancy, the chance to draw back, always ineffectiveness . . . that the moment one definitely commits oneself, then Providence moves too. A whole stream of events issues from the decision . . . which no man would have dreamt would have come his way.

– William Hutchison Murray[108]

Usually when we want to find beauty in a room we bring in many fancy things: furniture, paintings, rugs, decorations. However, to find what we are looking for it is better to take everything out of the room. When it is empty, its original beauty appears. When we take everything out of the room, we are saying no to whatever is in that the room that we don't want. We are emptying the room of all decoration to return it to its original form. I absolutely love garbage day! The people who pick it up may not like the weight of what I am saying no to, but the joy of doing so makes me certain it's the right thing to do.

Chapter 10

Approaching the Challenging Person with Love

When you feel you have to win the argument, prove the other wrong, or be better than them, you are approaching a challenging conversation from a fear-based scarcity consciousness paradigm.

This presents itself in the feeling that there is never enough praise, success, or money to go around, that you have quickly to grab whatever is good, taking it from others. Yet, no matter how much you get it's never enough. And when someone else receives something, you believe there's that much less for you. If they win, you lose.

In this mental set, it's easy to block out how enormously abundant the universe is, always replenishing itself and giving more. In fact, there is never a lack of praise, success, relationships, or supply of any kind. When one person receives, no one else is poorer for it. There is always enough for all. Those embedded in scarcity consciousness project their sense of fundamental emptiness on the world. They have forgotten their true place in life, and they have especially forgotten that God is love—however they envision and define their higher power.

Each of us has a higher nature filled with good will and compassion that knows the world is plentiful, and that it's impossible to lose anything that is really yours. The more you live in your higher nature, the less you will be subject to fear. As you break free from fear's power over you, your higher nature takes over and guides your behaviour during a challenging conversation, and in fact throughout your entire life. When we become friends and resolve conflicts, everyone wins. It is a necessity within any challenging conversation to avoid rivalry, a craving to be better than the other. Power struggles between leaders may be familiar, but they are no substitute for love.

All conflict stems from the idea that there can only be one winner, only one person or point of view that can be right. But true success comes from learning what it means to win together, to become friends. A great step in breaking the chains of fear is to leave power struggles behind and be able to win together all of the time.

Inner conflicts and conflicts with others are two sides of the same coin.

When you do not know who you are and what you truly need, not only do you live in conflict, you think that winning over others leads to well-being and success. You think that fighting leads to peace. It never happens; fighting leads to more fighting. Beating others out eventually leads to being beaten out. It cannot be any other way.

Win-win relationships are based upon mutual support and success. One person does not have to lose for another to win. Each only wins when the other does. An example of a win-win relationship is a man drowning in the ocean and someone jumping in to save him. They both must win together. The success of one is the success of both.

Shoshanna further illustrates the principle in a discussion of an event at the Seattle Special Olympics in 2004, when nine contestants, each physically or mentally disabled, assembled at the starting line for the 100-yard dash. At the gun, they all started out, not exactly in a dash, but with relish, to run the race to the finish and win.

All, that is, except one boy, who stumbled on the asphalt, tumbled over a couple of times, and began to cry. The other eight heard the boy cry. They slowed down and looked back. They all then turned around and went back. Each one of them.

One girl, who had Down syndrome, bent down, kissed him, and said, "This will make it better." All nine linked arms and walked across the finish line together. Everyone in the stadium stood and the cheering went on for over seven minutes. People who were there are still telling the story. Why? Because deep down we know one thing: what matters in this life is more than winning for ourselves. What truly matters is helping others win, even if it means slowing down and changing our course.

In order to build a win-win environment, misunderstandings must be dealt with on the spot. When misunderstandings are allowed to fester, they create havoc. Resentments build, obsessions grow, and relationships become tangled. Take charge of communications, respond to what you've heard—or what you think you've heard. Do it now, particularly as the now is all we have.

Remember, there may be worlds between what you've heard and what the other person actually meant. Feedback is crucial. Many of us are too proud to ask for feedback or to give it. We immediately assume we know what has been said. Most of the time we are off course.

As soon as any misunderstanding develops, realize that miscommunication is at the bottom of it. A feedback loop is required. This can instantly short-circuit bad feelings. If you notice that there's been a misunderstanding, say, "I would like to clarify what I think I heard you say." Then the other person can communicate what it was he or she heard.

Simply the willingness to clarify the communication and not blame the other person is an overt act of friendship and good will—of love—and is usually responded to as such. It gives you the opportunity to make corrections. From here further communication invariably takes place naturally.

Often a misunderstanding arises due to disappointment. When someone disappoints you, a common response is to withdraw and become unwilling to communicate.

Quickly communicating what is true for you in a situation has magical effects. Difficult conversations are required mainly when delays in communication have caused festering and allowed fear to creep in as a result. Nike is right: just do it!

Three true stories illustrating the benefits of approaching the challenging person with love

Story #1

During the twenty-nine years I was involved in training teachers I focused my research on attempting to find out why 18 percent of first-year high school teachers in Toronto quit their career within six months of beginning the profession.

I spent hundreds of hours observing young teachers (twenty-two to twenty-four years of age) from behind one-way mirrors. They were not aware that their classroom behaviour was being recorded and analyzed. The high school classes deliberately chosen were those of typically low socio-economic students ranging from fourteen to eighteen years old.

I shall never forget one particularly aggressive scenario when a first-year female mathematics teacher was confronted with a potentially violent male student of unusually large proportions for his fifteen years of age. John, whom the remainder of the class referred to as "Butch," was sitting in the front row, probably to facilitate control by the teachers whom he regularly terrorized.

The following was the sequence of verbal and non-verbal behaviours recorded. We later realized that this escalating sequence was particularly common to the 18 percent of teachers who quit and gave up their dream to be a teacher.

The teacher says, "OK, class, do the first three problems on page 12 in the text."

Butch turns to page 12, violently rips it out, crumples it in his large right hand, and throws it to the floor directly at the teacher's feet, while making sure the remainder of the class could hear the words: "This is bullshit. Make me."

The teacher steps backward and appears speechless.

Butch steps forward and escalates his aggressive confrontation, yelling, "F---ing bitch!"

The teacher steps back another two steps and bursts into tears.

Butch draws a six-inch knife from his right pant leg.

The teacher screams and runs out of the classroom door, never to return to any classroom as a teacher.

Story #2

Scenario: I am delivering a workshop to the senior leadership team of a mid-sized, privately owned manufacturing company in Saskatchewan, Canada.

My perception was that the eight executives sitting in front of me were responding enthusiastically to the topic "Leadership With Influence."

The CEO suddenly left the room, cell phone in hand, several minutes before the break we had planned at 10:30 a.m. I chose to say nothing, but I'm sure all present saw him depart abruptly. While I felt annoyed and even offended by his not even asking to be excused or making any comment at all, I let it go and carried on with my delivery and dialogue.

Approximately five minutes later, and still before 10:30 a.m., he reappeared, moved back to his seat, and still said nothing. Again, I am sure everyone was aware of his return but, like me, said nothing. After all, he's the CEO and his position of power probably justified his behaviour.

My teaching continued for another couple of minutes, and as I attempted to summarize with a thought-provoking pearl of wisdom to close the morning's agenda, Mr. CEO blurts out, "That's f---ing bullshit!"

I remember hearing a gasp from the majority of the team, and, predictably, all eyes suddenly flipped back to me. Nobody said so out loud, but I'm confident they were as shocked as I was, and instantly wondered *Wow! How's Denis going to handle such an unprofessional and violent confrontation?*

In hindsight, I now believe the three behaviours I demonstrated were not only critical steps for successfully dealing with difficult conversations, but were a consequence of studying the behaviours of first-year teachers who failed to deal successfully with challenging conversations.

> **Step 1:** I took a step toward the CEO, thus not giving him encouragement to escalate the disruptive behaviour in the manner shown by Butch.

> **Step 2:** I instantly adopted a mental set of caring to confront, and illustrated *dialogue* (no judgment) as opposed to *discussion* (a forcible striking of one object/word against another). As I recall, my actual words were: "Wow! Brian [not his real name], you sound really upset." I had studied this topic for years, and more importantly had practised, practised, practised empathetic behaviours from a mental set of love so many times that my Step 2 was now a habitual, automatic response to being thrown the hand grenade of a challenging conversation.

I knew it was paramount that I let Brian know that I understood him, particularly on an emotional level. Abraham Maslow, still regarded as a world authority on human needs and motivation, points out that "The deepest need of the human soul is the longing to be understood." I empathetically showed Brian that in this challenging conversation I was first seeking to understand him before having him understand me.

Brian paused and allowed me then to move to the next step, albeit a risky one.

> **Step 3:** I stepped back, looked at the whole team and asked, "Who else thinks that the material is a waste of time?" The risk here, of course, is that I am opening myself up to being told by others— maybe everyone—that I'm failing miserably.

Such vulnerability is an important leadership characteristic, as I would much prefer to be given feedback that I'm wasting my customer's time rather than not realize it.

Fortunately for my ego's sake, the team's response to my question and invitation to shoot me down, as Brian had demonstrated, was an immediate and overwhelming flood of affirming statements about my workshop material, all of which were in sharp contrast to Brian's obnoxious outburst.

I now had support from everyone else as I moved to resolve the conflict and conclude the challenging conversation.

At this point Brian stood up, apologized profusely, and asked if I'd mind if he explained where he was coming from. I encouraged him to take the floor and comment.

He again apologized to everyone present and went on to explain the profound significance of the phone call he had taken outside the meeting room. Apparently a most urgent business crisis had just threatened the whole organization, and so my working agenda was immediately postponed.

The potentially challenging conversation had been resolved relatively easily.

To this day, I still have a positive relationship with Brian and the whole organization. Having been asked to return for additional consulting work with the team is proof of the practical benefits of the three steps to challenging conversations.

By the way, the extensive research findings on the topic of habit formation[92] consistently point to the well-documented suggestion that a new behaviour does not become a habit until it is repeated for a minimum of twenty to twenty-four times. Some researchers such as M. Scott Peck[93] even suggest thirty times as a minimum.

Hence, a New Year's resolution to eat healthily will not likely be accomplished until the practice of choosing healthy foods every day of January is adopted.

Story#3

This is an experience I shall never forget. It involves Mr. John Irving, the CEO of J.D. Irving Limited. This conglomerate of a companies, based in the Canadian Maritimes, is the largest privately owned organization in the country and comprises many industries, including forest products, oil refineries, ship-building, pulp and paper mills, and mining. J.D. Irving himself is the largest single landowner in the provinces of New Brunswick and Nova Scotia, as well as the state of Maine. Not only is Mr. Irving a prestigious business leader, but he happens to be approximately six feet seven inches tall, a distinguished man of physical as well as business-leadership stature.

A colleague of mine (whom I shall call Michael) and I were co-presenting a four-day workshop on communication to a group of managers from the company. Michael was sitting in the back of the room while I took the responsibility of presenting a particular unit on the topic of effective presentation skills.

Unfortunately, Mr. Irving appeared at the door, and predictably the workshop participants all respectfully stood to applaud and welcome him in.

He gracefully accepted my invitation to say a few words and took over centre stage. His speech was perhaps only seven to eight minutes long, but during his delivery I noticed that the front three rows of vice presidents would physically rock back in their chairs whenever he would forcefully point at them with his index finger while emphasizing the key points of his speech. This caught my attention, as it happened to be one of the points I had been stressing with the course participants just minutes before the CEO appeared.

I had specifically warned to use an open palm when gesturing to another person, and to reserve the index finger only when pointing at an inanimate object, or if you are referring to #1. I had argued that pointing to others with the index finger usually generates defensiveness rather than buy-in, listening, or followership. Here was the country's most prominent business leader giving me a golden opportunity to comment on the very point I had mentioned just seconds before he took over.

Mr. Irving gained a strong round of applause in response to his forceful delivery, and I thought I'd seize the opportunity to involve him, and all the participants, with the content of my own presentation.

At the point when I began to add my thanks to the CEO and ask him publicly if I could make a comment on his delivery style, I noticed my colleague sitting in the back giving me passionate non-verbal signals to stop. Michael was not using words but waving his hand in front of his throat as if to say, *Stop it, you'll cut your own throat, and probably mine too, if you go where I think you're going.*

Too late. I had already begun the potentially challenging conversation. At least I had begun by asking permission, and, predictably, Mr. Irving said, "Yes, certainly."

I stepped toward him (as I'd learned from the above case study) and simply illustrated with my right hand the difference between pointing at someone with one's index finger in comparison to the open palm. Then I said, "Did you notice, Mr. Irving, that when you pointed at the senior managers in front of you they all literally rocked back in their chairs? Perhaps they took your instruction as a threatening demand?"

He replied, "Oh, Dr. Shackel, thank you. I'd never thought of this before. I'll remember that."

He departed to his waiting plane to yet another round of applause from all present—especially from Michael and me.

What truly impressed me, though, was that when I happened to meet Mr. Irving again at a function held at Ivey Business School eight months later, he saw me, smiled, and extended his open palm in a warm greeting: "Oh, Mr. Shackel, how are you doing?"

We both laughed, and have been on positive terms ever since.

Chapter 11

Release Attachments

As a rule, whatever is fluid, soft, and yielding will overcome whatever is rigid and hard.

– Tao Te Ching

We too often live with the incredible idea that everything will and should stay the same. We cling to this notion for dear life and are continually surprised when the things we love leave, wonderful relationships fade, our body changes, people behave in unexpected ways, or our fortunes fluctuate. When all of this happens, as it naturally must, we may even feel personally insulted or betrayed: "How can this be happening to me!" Others feel victimized by change, as if it's living proof that they are failures. They have failed to hold everything together, to keep things the same. They have failed to have their expectations realized—expectations which did not factor in the inevitable process of change.

A Taoist story tells of an old man who accidentally fell into the river rapids leading to a dangerous waterfall. Onlookers feared for his life. Miraculously, he came out alive and unharmed downstream, at the bottom of the falls. People asked him how he managed to survive.

"I accommodated myself to the water, not the water to me. Without thinking, I allowed myself to be shaped by it. Plunging into the swirl, I came out with the swirl. This is how I survived." Going with the flow involves letting go and letting God.

However, many of us do not feel that change is beautiful and thrilling. They find it frightening, resist it, and do all they can to block it out. They set up dams to hold it back, rigid beliefs and ideas that seek to contain the flow.

But if not for the process of constant change, no growth would be possible. Your experience of yourself and others could not deepen. You would not be able to tell the difference between childish infatuation and real love. Without change, a child could not go from sitting to crawling, and then from crawling to walking. They would remain an infant forever. Their life would not be fulfilled. Change is your friend. Change is a gift. It is crucial to learn to see it that way.

Fear, however, has a different plan. Fear says that change is dangerous, and security comes from holding on to what's familiar, to the past. The old ways are right and new ways are wrong. You must hold on to what you learned in childhood, and what your family believed. Fear basically advises you not to grow up. The Danish philosopher Søren Kierkegaard wisely said that most people never grow beyond the age of fifteen, apart from chronologically. They do not develop a sense of inquiry, inner independence, and openness to change. Instead they conform to old patterns and endlessly repeat the mistakes of the past. This is what Freud would have called "repetition compulsion," and it involves unconsciously drawing the same situation to yourself or reliving the same relationship over and over again. Such situations won't turn out differently, because you aren't different. Until you change, the regiments of old patterns, beliefs, and expectations hold sway.

A woman was asked, "Why are you sitting in front of a bowl of sour pickles, which obviously make you cry and pull that terrible face? Why do you keep eating one sour pickle after the other?"

"Because I'm waiting for a sweet one."

Mmmmm!

The woman had obviously become caught in repetition compulsion and had become rigid, a prisoner of fear.

Fear warns, preventing us from exploring new possibilities. It warns us to love only within one particular social, ethnic, or religious group, and to be wary of others. People who are different are considered dangerous. We must regard them with suspicion and keep them at arm's length.

A common story: a new family, with different colour skin and a severely disabled child, moved into an upscale neighbourhood, excited to meet the others. A wave of alarm spreads over the neighbourhood and doors shut promptly. Those inside vigilantly guard themselves, their families, and their beliefs, never getting to know the new people, the gifts they brought with them, or the ways their lives could have been enhanced by them. Neither did they know how much pain they caused the family.

However, when we cause pain, knowingly or unknowingly, we give fear a chance to grow. From deep within, we expect retaliation, or find some ways to punish ourselves. What is the line from the Eagles' most famous song, "Hotel California"?

We are all just prisoners here of our own device.

It's absolutely crucial to keep looking at the insidious ways fear distorts what could be a hopeful, joyous, thoroughly satisfying life into one of shut-upness and dread. As soon as you let a little light in, it is easy to notice that there are many cracks in fear's facade.

> *There is a crack in everything, that's how the light gets in.*
>
> – Leonard Cohen

> *Dwelling as change itself brings peace.*
>
> – Buddhist Teaching

If we could change ourselves, the tendencies in the world would also change. As a man changes his own nature, so does the attitude of the world change towards him.

— Mahatma Gandhi[94]

Because the central importance of caring is stressed throughout this book and we have already introduced the importance of love, it seems relevant to point to The Love Project, which is the title of a chapter within a work by the educator Arleen Lorrance.[95] She stresses that: "One way to start a preventive program is to be the change you want to see happen."

Most of us resist change because it feels like loss. But change is not loss, it is simply change; it is inevitable, healthy, and necessary. Rather than see change as bringing new life and growth, it's easy to see it as a villain, taking something you've loved away. However, if something truly belongs to you, nothing can take it away. If something does not belong to you, no matter how hard you cling to it, it still must go where it belongs.

Freedom's just another word for nothin' left to lose.

— Kris Kristofferson, "Me and Bobby McGee"

All composite things must, one day, decompose.

— Diamond Sūtra

Two Zen monks were in the forest when they saw a beautiful woman in distress. She was lost and needed help finding her way home. They took her along with them, and soon came to a deep stream. One of the monks picked her up and carried her

across. After they crossed the stream, he put her
down, and guided her to the right road.

The two monks continued on. Finally, after about an hour
of walking, one monk said to the one who had lifted the woman,
"You know, we are not allowed to touch a woman. Yet you picked
that woman up and carried her in your arms."

"Yes, I did," said the other monk. "But I have put her down,
and you are still carrying her with you now."[96]

When you put down whatever you have been carrying, you
can walk along freely without guilt and obstructions. Physically,
it's easy to put a woman down, but more difficult to drop thoughts
and fantasies you carry about her. But the more of our inner
baggage we put down, the lighter and freer our trip through life
will be.

Welcome whatever comes into your world today, even if you
didn't plan for it, or if it seems unwanted. If it is there, welcome
it. Don't fight it off. Instead, be thankful for it being present. As
you do so, you will become available to deal with challenging
conversations in a truly different way.

Some crave so much that no matter what they have, they
cannot be satisfied. In Chinese Buddhism this is called being
a hungry ghost: being run by the affliction of greed.[97] When a
hungry ghost is invited to a banquet, he samples everything, eats
it up, but cannot taste, savour, or digest the delicious meal in front
of him. No matter what he eats, he is left hungrier than before.

Similarly, when a hungry ghost is invited to the banquet of
life, he cannot taste or digest his experiences. A hungry ghost
can be hungry for food, love, money, sex, recognition, anything.
Whatever he receives he wants more. The hungry ghost does not
realize that it is greed that causes the pain. And the more he grasps,
the more he crushes whatever he has in the palm of his hands. As
you learn to let go rather than feed your cravings, the hunger and
fear will subside.

As you feed your cravings, you become controlled by the desire to search for and cling to whatever feels good and reject whatever feels threatening. When you find what you like, you become attached, and when you find what you dislike, you use all your power to push it away. Thus, you spend your precious life energy discarding half your experience and grasping and clinging to the rest. Living in this way, you become completely dependent upon external conditions for your sense of well-being. A sunny day will make you happy, but as soon as thunderstorms arrive your happiness is gone. Like a leaf blown in the wind, you can't relax, and are always on guard about what's coming next. Because people and conditions constantly change, you have no idea what you can really hold on to, or where to find true security.

You may think something painful is bad for you, and something that feels good is positive. But this is not so. You may be rejecting something that could be meaningful, because it initially makes you uneasy. You may be staying attached to something that is harmful simply because it is familiar. It's impossible to realize what is truly beneficial when you live in this way.

Deep within ourselves we do not allow life to be what it is. We judge, condemn, and refuse life in many subtle ways. Fear enjoys harming life. Do not go along with its destructive wishes. There is never, ever anything good that comes out of creating harm. Extricate yourself from this activity. Claim a different desire. When you feel the desire to harm or reject, realize this desire does not belong to you. It belongs to fear. You do not have to go along with fear's madness.

Chapter 12

Intuition

You will never follow your own inner voice until you clear up the doubts in your mind.

— Roy Bennett[98]

All human knowledge begins with intuitions, proceeds from thence to concepts, and ends with ideas.

— Immanuel Kant[118]

Our bodies have five senses: touch, smell, taste, sight, and hearing. But not to be overlooked or underestimated in importance is the main sense of the soul: intuition.

Albert Einstein stated that "the only really valuable thing is intuition."

The futurist Joel Barker defined intuition as "the ability to solve problems with insufficient data,"[99] but Ingrid Bergman acknowledged that intuition does need training: "You must trust your intuition. You must trust the small voice inside which tells you exactly what to say, what to decide."

When unexpected events come into your life, it's easy to lose your bearings. Unprepared for sudden change and gripped by fear, the world no longer seems safe or secure. You wonder when the next shoe is going to fall, or who you can really trust. You may feel you cannot depend on others, or on yourself, either. When your certainty is shaken it can be difficult to determine what is real and what is not. At this juncture it's easy to retreat into fantasies. The truth is that although these fantasies seem to bring comfort, they disconnect you from what is actually happening, from workable solutions and true peace of mind.

The world of fantasies is a world we live in, automatically and unknowingly. As soon as something happens that is difficult to cope with—a desire obstructed, a relationship threatened—we retreat into fantasies in order to regain equilibrium and get power over our world.

Fantasies, on the surface, seem to comfort, soothe hurt feelings, calm us temporarily and make us feel that all is well. Some fantasies create an explanation for what might have happened. Others provide wished for outcomes, as though the situation is being handled and you are victorious. Usually you are vindicated in your fantasies, a winner. You find the love you've been looking for, reclaim your pride, do away with enemies.

In other fantasies you may see yourself as a hapless victim. These fantasies reinforce negative beliefs, distorting the reality of who you are and what has really gone on.

Dwelling in fantasies is dangerous. Although they may seem to be a comfort initially, they are based on fear. By drawing you away from reality, by keeping your energies tied up in wishful thinking, the basic situation that has caused your upset is never faced or handled. In fact, because it is not being attended to, the situation often intensifies, festers, and grows.

It can be very shocking to realize that a fantasy is a falsehood. They can become so intense that they feel like reality. By replaying them over and over, your fantasies begin to feel like old friends. When fantasies become very familiar, rather than paying attention to what's going on, you simply enjoy your fantasies and neglect the many warnings, signs, and messages life is presenting about the truth of the situation you're involved in. Then, when things escalate, when the harsh truth appears and you're suddenly fired, or your relationship abruptly ends, the shock can be enormous. You had no idea this was coming because you simply weren't available to hear or see what was going on in your own life.

By drawing your attention away from the actual situation, fantasies make you deaf and blind. No matter what is in front of your eyes, you cannot see it. You see only your fantasy about it. No matter what is being said, you don't really hear. You may hear only a portion of what is being communicated and distort the rest. Your fantasies filter in information you want to hear and filter out whatever doesn't fit in with your desires.

A huge part of becoming fearless is developing the ability to recognize what reality brings you, and not getting lost in a mirage. When you are able to recognize what's happening, you will simultaneously find real ways of responding to what's being asked of you.

Am I saying that fantasy and visioning is fear-based and bad for our sanity, as well as solve problems successfully? Definitely not!

In fact, if it was not for envisioning the rising sun during the night of May 17, 1997, while stuck at the top of Mount Ruapehu I would have died. I am unequivocally certain of that.

The chapter on vision in *Five Seconds at a Time* affirms the truth of what leaders already know: "Where there is no vision, people perish" (Prov 29:18).

Yes, of course, leaders, organizations, and teams need vision to know where they're going, but the big question is: Is your vision negative or positive; fear-based or love-based?

While shaking uncontrollably on the floor of the hut at 8,000 feet in minus-30-degree temperatures and wearing very little clothing, I repeatedly caught myself experiencing an extremely painful wave of fear that I was going to die. I firmly believe that repeatedly choosing to switch to seeing the rising sun saved the day, and in fact every day since.

Easy? No.

Important? Undeniably. Indubitably!

Accepting the reality that I was in a particularly serious predicament was the beginning, but the end was accomplished only because I had the self-discipline to focus my fantasies on survival, not death.

It's worth repeating my maxim that "what you focus on is amplified."

- Strive for what you want, not what you don't want.
- Choose good over bad.
- Look for and therefore see the strength of your partner or colleague, and not the weaknesses.
- The fear-based paradigm of thinking will kill you!

Everyday reality brings so many opportunities, guidance, and unexpected gifts. Are you available to receive them, or are you lost in a fantasy about what should happen, how the world should treat you?

When fear-based fantasies take over, obsessive thinking is not far behind. Obsessive, repetitive thinking is designed to tie you in a knot. When you're caught in the grip of obsessive thinking—in an attempt to come to terms with the blows you've been dealt or to ensure that all will go as you wish in the future—your mind replays the same events over and over again, never finding a solution.

Obsessive thinking develops naturally into obsessive-compulsive behaviour. Rather than face the reality of how out of control you feel, you now substitute repetitive behaviours and rituals to produce a feeling of stability and safety. The price you pay for this is enormous. Repetitive behaviours not only limit your life, they take enormous time and energy to keep going. Not only do they take your freedom away, but the sense of safety they produce is fragile. As soon as a ritual is not performed, or a certain behaviour is not engaged in, fear arises once again.

Remember: fear is a bully and trickster generating self-imposed and crippling cages of limitations on us.

> Cynthia could not forgive either herself or her father for the terrible abuse she had suffered at his hands. She had no idea, either, how to cleanse herself or feel worthwhile again. At first, she began washing her hands after every meal, feeling it wiped the shame away. Soon, it wasn't enough to wash after every meal; she began washing between meals as well. That felt even better, but when she forgot to do it, anxiety arose. Before long, she also had to wash whenever she was out in public. The compulsion was taking control of her life and she felt terrified when she forgot. Maria couldn't understand why the more she washed the more she needed to.

Obsessive-compulsive rituals soothe anxiety temporarily. But, unless the source of the anxiety is faced and released, it remains, lurking beneath the surface. Cynthia's compulsion was a defense against feelings she had related to the abuse. She had no idea how to free herself from these feelings and was symbolically washing away the pain she felt. However, in the long run, as obsessive behaviour and rituals take over, they restrict and impair our lives and fuel addictions of all kinds. Ultimately they cause more anxiety and dis-ease.

To a degree, all of us seek to control fear through routines, rituals, and automatic patterns that don't let go. The more we indulge them, however, the more frightening reality can seem, and the less able we are to take effective action.

Chapter 13

Navigate to a Safe Harbour

*Boats are designed to get out and ride the open seas,
not to rot in harbour.*

— Denis Shackel

The opening three words in Chapter 1 of *The Road Less Traveled* by M. Scott Peck 93 immediately resonated with me as soon as I picked it up: "Life is difficult!"

Amen to that! I couldn't put the book down until I had read it.

So are conversations frequently difficult, and as a result trigger our loss of equilibrium and peace of mind.

> Bailey overheard negative comments being made about her by her co-workers. She wasn't exactly sure what they were saying, however, because they became very quiet when she walked by. This allowed her fear-driven imagination to run wild and caused her to feel anxious and alone. Then, in turn, Bailey began speaking about those co-workers to others. Before long she found herself caught in a vicious cycle of suspicion and ill will.

There are conversational terrorists out there, just waiting to fill you with gossip, negative rumours, and fear. If you do not know what's happening, you may not realize that you're being harmed, and you'll have no defenses against it or know how to make it stop. At this point, a general sense of anxiety arises and you often end up handling it in dysfunctional ways.

Even your personal relationships with people you trust and hold dear can become unpredictable. A crisis may occur when a friend says something cruel or you become the butt of a joke or an insult. In the midst of a wonderful relationship, a jealous person can intrude and attempt to destroy the relationship. This kind of personal, emotional pain can be harder to bear than physical suffering.

Most of us do not know how to deal with painful emotions and instead turn to drink, drugs, and diversions of all kinds to put an end to them. But these ways of resisting pain cause more fear and pain in the long run.

In order to find true freedom from pain there is a fundamental assumption that must be questioned. It is the idea that pain is terrible and must be avoided at all costs. Usually, as soon as you start to feel pain you immediately try to make it go away. You'll do anything to find a way to change, soothe, or suppress what you're going through. But if you stop, even for a little while, it's easy to see that lasting comfort doesn't come that way.

All life involves suffering; this is inevitable. This statement has been thought to be pessimistic. The opposite is true. The statement does not suggest that you fear life, shut down, or refuse your experience. By learning how to interact with it wisely, you have the possibility of ending your suffering once and for all.

The definition of "responsibility" is the ability to respond. Many of us do not yet have that ability—we just react. When you react, you are easily affected by everything—events, people, and your interpretations of what's going on. You become like a puppet, flailing in the wind. Someone says something nasty and you become filled with hurt; someone else says something seductive, and you fall under their spell. Reactions are automatic and impulsive, and seldom bring wisdom or healing in their wake. Responses are different.

In our search for safety and freedom from pain, most of us spend a huge amount of time and energy trying to change people. That's a waste of time. You can't change what the other person is doing, but you can take charge of your reactions and learn instead how to respond. It is not people or situations that are producing fear and pain, but your *reactions* to them. This cannot be emphasized often enough.

As you become aware of your negative reactions and dissolve them, you are no longer at the mercy of conditions and individuals. You can go where you like and be at ease with whatever happens, and whoever is there. How you respond is in your hands.

Realize that people rarely attack others unless they are hurting and in pain themselves. The person who has attacked you is expressing his own fear. You do not have to accept this person's hurtful comments as the truth. Refuse to take in the other person's poison and stay planted in the truth of who you are. You do not have to be dependent upon others for your sense of self-worth.

Most of us long for conditions to be different. You feel you must change life, overpower it with all your ideas about how everything should turn out for *you*. This self-preoccupation may be called the pain of arrogance, the idea that everything revolves around your personal needs and that the whole world exists to suit *you*.

You may be in a relationship that tastes sweet and you don't notice the ways in which it weakens and undermines your life. On the other hand, a person, job, or situation may taste bitter, be initially difficult, and this situation can be beneficial in all kinds of ways. Struggling with a difficult person or circumstance can strengthen you, allow you to tap into your courage and strength. You may think you are up against danger and harm, but the situation might be a gift in disguise.

Most of the time, however, we decide what is good or bad based upon whether we like it or not, whether it tastes bitter or sweet—but this is a limited perspective.

Look more deeply at what is truly beneficial in your life, and what really causes distress or harm. When you look only for sweetness, when you avoid bitterness or pain, you are strengthening the illness, increasing fear in your life. When you are willing to engage with all of your experience, to taste the bitter and the sweet, you are taking a medicine that ultimately makes you stronger. How much power can fear have in your life when you are willing to accept your pain? When you are willing to take whatever comes, fear can no longer keep you living a small, secluded, shut-down life.

Pain is not suffering. It is just pain. You cut your finger and it throbs. You become ill and your body aches. A dear friend dies and you mourn. These are natural life circumstances that cannot be avoided. They are not to be feared but taken for what they are.

We often turn pain into suffering, which is even harder to cope with. At the beginning of Mandela's imprisonment, when he hated and fought everything that was going on, he suffered greatly. When he accepted the situation for what it was, he began to find ways to grow inside it. His cell turned into an art studio; his imprisonment turned into a journey toward a life of real worth.

The way we turn pain into suffering is to dwell upon it and make it mean something terrible, blame others for it, talk about it to everyone, use it to get sympathy and attention. We feel we are being singled out for unfair treatment or become victims or martyrs. When we engage in this kind of behaviour, suffering becomes a way of life. This kind of suffering can become addictive.

Reality is not your enemy, but it certainly can become the enemy of your expectations. You start a business and expect it to succeed in a year or two; you choose a life partner and expect to be happy the rest of your life; you enter a race and are sure you are going to win. You are trained to see all of life through the lens of your expectations. You are even told that certain people are good and others are bad—and you expect it to be true.

Needless to say, reality often brings experiences that contradict these deeply held beliefs. Each time this happens, fear develops. What is important to see is that it is not reality, but your *expectations* that are causing the trouble. When you allow reality to manifest, you grow safe and strong.

Letting go of expectations does not mean you let go of your standards, values, or boundaries. It simply means that as you let go of expectations you develop the flexibility to take appropriate actions and make choices that are constructive. When you cling to false expectations, you get tied up in anger, struggle, and heartache, sometimes rejecting those you care for the most. These expectations are a suit of armour that does not really protect you, it just provides another way of becoming numb.

It is very important to distinguish between *constructive* and *destructive* challenges. Sometimes you create repetitive challenges that are based upon your desire to suffer and live in fear. Other challenges are based upon your desire to overcome fear, grow strong and brave, and enjoy life fully. Distinguish between these two kinds of challenges in your life. Draw a line in the middle of a page and write each kind down on either side.

The challenges that are positive and healthy for you are part of the journey to becoming fearless. Even though you experience difficulty, pain, or failure along the way, by forging ahead the fear will diminish and you will grow.

The challenges that are repetitive, obsessive, and make you weak are destructive, counterfeit challenges. They are substitutes for the real thing. These challenges may create a false high, or excitement, but usually they are based in a situation where you cannot win, or where someone else will be in pain—gambling with your family's income, for example, or being in a volatile relationship, or refusing to seek medical care even though you are ill. These challenges do not produce strength or well-being because they arise from a love of danger, an attachment to suffering, or a desire to receive or inflict harm. See these challenges for what they are and let them go.

I wrote this chapter aboard a flight to Saskatoon to present a workshop. During the hour before I boarded the plane, I was deeply disturbed by watching a few minutes of a CBC television program. It presented data that are true in my chosen country of Canada. In this country there are hundreds of women who, after being raped and murdered, were found in the Red River and the Assiniboine River close to Winnipeg.

They are invariably First Nations women. According to those being interviewed, the predominantly white RCMP officers turned the other way.

One particular woman stated, "We all know about the social discrimination in the United States, but we Canadians are actually worse. We refuse to even talk about it."

Reality always brings what is needed, whether you like it or not. The more you welcome what is being brought to you—feel it, taste it, know it—the more you release false expectations and are able to absorb the lessons you need to learn. Then you can open your treasure house, access your enormous inner resources, and receive the plentiful nourishment and support that is waiting for you.

Chapter 14

Generate Caring

*Let your fellow's honour be as dear to you as your
own and do not anger easily.*

– Johanan Ben Zakkai,
first-century Jewish sage

Self-hatred is one of the main illnesses of today. It's little wonder
increasing numbers of books and psychological services are about
anger management. When this illness strikes it often manifests as
depression, which is anger turned against the Self. It arises when
you have not been given permission by yourself or anyone else
to express yourself constructively. Repressed anger festers within
and finally turns against you as you punish yourself in all kinds
of ways. Although this may not be done consciously, it happens
nonetheless.

People who are in the grip of self-hatred have a negative
and fragile sense of themselves. They crave respect and approval
and often choose partners, jobs, and lifestyles that are socially
acceptable. In this way they feel as though they are respectable
and fit in. However, when their cover is threatened and their
vulnerabilities and problems come to light, not only does self-
hatred emerge, but hatred of others as well.

The Canadian Oxford Dictionary defines *malevolent* as
"having or showing a wish to do evil with others."

The malevolent mind is fuelled by the poison of anger. It is unable to stop for a moment and take note of what it is feeling or how it behaves. It is a mind that has lost perspective; once it takes over there is no end to the damage it creates. In some cases it becomes focused on revenge, at other times on dominating and getting its way. What a dramatic and disturbing consequence of choosing to be motivated by and operating from a paradigm of fear!

When you feel threatened, attacked, or not properly valued, the malevolent mind tells you that attacking in return will make you safe or restore your wounded pride. But it doesn't—the opposite is true. Attacking in return makes you more fearful of repercussions and takes your self-respect away. Hatred has no respect for us. Just like an autoimmune disease, where the body attacks its own organs, hatred eats up our well-being. People in the grip of the self-created malevolent mind can easily become prey to alcohol or drugs and spin out of control, which can even cause serious health conditions such as heart attacks, strokes, and cancer.

Flying home from my consulting trip to Saskatoon, what comes to my attention in today's Globe and Mail but an article in the Life and Arts section entitled "Moving Towards Cancer." Diagnosed with "lazy" cancer that is treatable but recurring, writer Aviva Rubin will never know the relief of being cancer-free. Anxiety and fear know no bounds to her post-chemo world as she tries to outrun lymphoma.

Aviva states, "Once I was a woman with a great fear of cancer. A woman who regularly went to second base with her GP and took innumerable ultrasounds in order to hear the words 'no cancer here' to diminish the pain the fear had inflated. Then one day the doctor reported that there was something malignant there and everything changed to a life when I will never know life without cancer. The diagnosis was lymphoma and I took a sharp turn into a bumpy road of chemotherapy, scans, painful invasive tests. More blood work more scans, more tests. I went from being anxious for no good reason to anxious with cause!"

Had Aviva now gotten cancer as a consequence of thought choice?

Interestingly, the very next article reports, "Landing on a comet, 317 million miles from home." It states, "Everything about the Rosetta mission to land on a comet is mind-blowing."

What I find even more mind-blowing is that we can attain truly extraordinary scientific accomplishments but fail to know how to start with ourselves and become aware of how Aviva's thought choice is blowing her whole body apart, not just her mind.

Am I saying her cancer is a result of her fear-ridden thought pattern? No, that seems like an exaggerated oversimplification.

Am I saying we can overcome cancer by taking responsibility for our freedom to choose a paradigm of love and health versus a paradigm of fear and disease? That too seems a gross oversimplification. Nonetheless, all disease is simply dis-ease, and an increasing number of medical research publications do point to the interrelation between mental and physical health.

The older I become, the more I become convinced that Henry Ford was correct when he said, and I paraphrase: whether you believe you will or you believe you won't get cancer, you're probably right.

Ford also said, "We become what we think."

If our thought choice is that fundamentally connected to our well-being and our success in personal and professional dealings with other people, then avoiding at all costs most certainly costs, perhaps our very lives.

But let's go back to the malevolent mind and see how it too is a thought choice, and obviously fuelled by fear.

When the malevolent mind becomes unstoppable, it crushes whatever stands in its way. In many respects it is like a wild animal on a feeding frenzy, not caring who the victim is. In its grip, you can harm those who are closest to you, especially yourself.

Of course, there are different degrees of malevolence and times when you can see the light and be reasoned with. Other times you cannot.

Actions taken as a result of anger are often thought to be expressions of strength. The sense of power you feel when attacking makes it seem as if what you are doing is undeniably right. However, after the hatred passes and you've left things worse than they were before, you usually feel weak and depleted. The rush that comes from anger is a substitute for real strength. Real strength requires that you have the ability to refuse the urging of the malevolent mind, the clarity to see the situation in its largest perspective, and the capacity to respond compassionately.

In this day and age, we see a proliferation of hatred and violence being acted out all over the world, and in the lives of many of us. All fear-based behaviour is the root cause of any challenging conversation, whether it's in a professional setting or a personal relationship. In order to get rid of this poison, it is not sufficient to deal with the branches, the expressions of anger, we must go to the roots and pull them out.

Prophets have for centuries given guidance in ways to uproot this poison, including the malevolent mind.

> *With gentleness overcome anger. With generosity overcome meanness. With truth overcome deceit.*
>
> – Buddha

> *Do not be overcome by evil, but overcome evil with good.*
>
> – St. Paul, Romans 12:21

But do we listen?

The Manataka American Indian Council works hard to preserve the culture of the American Indian. As a result, the following classic tale, told many times around the sacred fire during ceremonies, is probably familiar to the reader. It is, however, well worth hearing yet again…

> A grandson came to his elderly grandfather, filled with anger because a so-called friend had deceived him and done him a great injustice. The grandfather said, "Let me tell you a story. I too at times have felt great hate for those who have taken so much, and feel no remorse for what they do. But hate wears you down and does not hurt your enemy. It's like taking poison and wishing your enemy would die.

"I have struggled with these feelings many times. It is as though there are two wolves inside me; one is good and does no harm. He lives in harmony with those around him and does not take offense. He will only fight when it is right to do so, and in the right way. But, the other wolf, ah! The littlest thing will send him into a fit of temper. He fights everyone, all of the time, for no reason. He cannot think because his anger and hate are so great. It is helpless anger, for it will change nothing.

"Sometimes it is hard to live with these two wolves inside me, for both of them try to dominate my spirit."

"Which one wins?" asked the boy.

"The one I feed," replied the wise man.

Even though you may not be aware of it, the malevolent mind has many ways of taking root and growing in your life. One powerful way is for it to tell you that you are right and others wrong; life is a battle and you have to win; others are your enemies; it does not matter who you crush on your way to the top of the ladder. The malevolent mind tells you that if someone hurts you,

you must hurt him back, twice as hard, to prevent this attack from ever repeating. The malevolent mind simply does not realize that any action taken in hatred does not stop the situation from happening; in fact, it ensures that it will.

You cannot find peace through attack. The more hatred you send to others, the more it returns to your own life. This is a basic law of life. It is irrefutable and constant. Those harmed will rise up, sooner or later, and get their revenge. These are the cycles of predictable destiny. How to put an end to them?

In order to dissolve fear, you have to work with the hatred in your own life. Because this feeling is so unacceptable to most of us and to society at large, usually anger and hatred go underground. You repress your hatred, smile nicely, and do all you can to act as though you are so spiritual or holy that anger never approaches you. However, anger approaches all of us. The malevolent mind is always there, waiting for an opportunity to flare up. In order to root it out of your life, you must first be willing to face it and acknowledge it for what it is.

When you do, a funny thing happens. Like fear, as soon as you look it in the eye and expose its lies, anger begins to wobble and fade away. It has no power on its own, just what you give it. When you believe the lies it tells, it metastasizes like cancer. However, when you are on the alert and say no, you are in effect pulling out the roots. The many ways of saying no to anger fill you with vitamins and minerals of the soul. They build up your spiritual immune system and make you strong.

One root of anger is the ongoing justification of it. Some people feel that it is natural, even healthy to be angry and to take it out on others. It's one thing to express anger in a healthy, responsible, constructive manner, and quite another to use it to attack, to blame others, condemn, deceive, etc. When you're involved in justifying your anger, you can find all kinds of theories, beliefs, and reasons to allow anger to rule your life.

Like most of us, you've also been taught to believe that if someone offends or insults you it is healthy to let them have a piece of your mind. If you don't, you'll become a doormat. Some people are always looking for insults and slights from others, just waiting for an opportunity to let their anger out.

There are many ways of responding to insults constructively that keep you from becoming sucked into a negative whirl. In fact, you can even approach the experience of being insulted as an opportunity to grow. But first you need to make the thought choice that being insulted can have a positive outcome. The insult may have come to you to help you build strength and endurance, to teach you not to respond impulsively. Perhaps you are being invited to develop compassion, to look more deeply at who the other person really is.

If you do not take the insult personally, it cannot hurt you at all. Simply realize that the person who insulted you had to be in pain to behave in that way. The insult simply shows you that he or she is in need of compassion and care. You could respond with kindness; you could offer understanding in return.

Here is a story from *Zen Stories of the Samurai*[100] about a different way of handling anger that arises.

> There was once a great warrior, and though he was still quite old, he was able to defeat any challenger. His reputation extended far and wide and many students came to study with him.
>
> One day an infamous young warrior arrived. He was determined to be the first one to defeat the great Master. Along with his strength, he had an uncanny ability to spot and exploit any weakness in an opponent. He would wait for his opponent to make the first move, thus revealing a weakness, and then would strike mercilessly with great speed. No one had ever lasted beyond the first move in a match with him.

Against the advice of his students, the old Master gladly accepted the young warrior's challenge. As the two squared off for battle, the young warrior began to hurl insults at the old Master. He threw dirt in his face. For hours he verbally assaulted him with every curse known to mankind. But the old warrior merely stood there, motionless and calm. Finally, the young warrior exhausted himself. Knowing he was defeated, he left shamed.

Somewhat disappointed that he did not fight the insolent young man, the students gathered around the old Master and questioned him. "How could you endure such an indignity? How did you drive him away?"

"If someone comes to give you a gift and you do not receive it," the Master replied, "to whom does the gift belong?"

The Master had conquered his own pride and self-importance and could therefore not be thrown off balance and harmed.

Another root of the malevolent mind is the idea that the world is divided into two camps: people are either good or bad. Of course, you are always in the right camp, and everyone else in the wrong one. And, of course, it's fine to hate those in the wrong camp, even to destroy them. Perhaps more than once you have proven your self-worth by declaring others bad or wrong.

False pride keeps us looking down on others, projecting our fears on them, not seeing who they truly are. It prevents us from behaving in ways that would be beneficial to all. When acting from false pride you do not stop to realize that the person you consider your enemy today may become your dearest friend tomorrow. Friends turn into enemies and enemies into friends all the time. We do not live in a black and white world. Change is constant, including a change of heart and mind.

That which you cannot accept in another is something you cannot accept in yourself.

Your shadow includes the repressed, unacceptable aspects of your nature that you have repressed, including attitudes, memories, or desires you cannot face or accept in yourself. It's much easier to see the negativity in others, hate and fight them for it, than to face these qualities in yourself. This shadow has a powerful influence and affects your life in all kinds of ways. As you have to keep it hidden, it drains energy from you, keeps you in conflict, and makes you generally miserable.

Once you face your shadow, your energy and well-being are freed up. Now you don't have to blame others for that which you cannot accept in yourself. This is called "eating your shadow." It is such an important concept that it is well worth stopping and really taking it in. If there is someone you hate, reject, or feel agitated by, realize that you have attracted this person to you and that he or she is simply showing you something you cannot accept in yourself.

The more you repress aspects of yourself and project them onto others, the more you will attract people who mirror them. Worst of all, when you refuse to face the shadow within, when you spend time projecting it on others, paranoia can develop. Then it becomes easy to feel the entire world as malevolent, plotting harm behind your back. Not only is this a projection of your own hatred, but it can also be an unconscious wish to be harmed.

Just because you're paranoid doesn't mean they aren't after you.

– Joseph Heller, *Catch 22*[101]

Paranoia is completely driven by fear. The truly paranoid individual is out of touch with reality, only imagining the worst, seeing danger, hearing a sneer, or sensing an attack behind every word spoken to him, and feeling like the entire world is out to get him. If a person is just casually grimacing, the paranoid immediately decides that the person is on the verge of an attack.

Everyone can be subject to paranoid moments, but there is a continuum here. At first, perhaps, it may last only for a few moments, but if you are not careful true paranoia can grow and take over your life. Paranoia is disabling because it prevents you from seeing the world clearly, decreases your options, intensifies fear, and peoples your world with enemies. It is crucial that you understand how it operates within professional organizations, even churches, and among nations, and how to undo it.

When paranoia strikes, you begin to attribute dark motives and suspect behaviour to others. You can become convinced you are confronting a dangerous enemy and have to remove them from your life. You do not see the shared humanity between you, only what is different. You do not realize that like you, this individual wants to be happy and avoid sorrow; that, like you, they have suffered and want to be safe; that one day, like you, they will face death.

When fear is activated, it is very easy for the paranoid mind to flourish. It is also easy to respond in a paranoid manner when confronted with individuals from another race, religion, or culture. Because these people are different and unfamiliar, it is easy to project the worst upon them. The more you see someone as an enemy, the more you allow the paranoid mind to grow, and the more you actually call those qualities out in the person. Perception is reality, perception is fatal. As you see others, so they respond.

We bring out in others what we see in them.

When you see the worst in a person, you send them an unconscious message about who they are to you, and unconsciously they fulfill that role. This dynamic operates on many levels: between parents and children, husband and wives, and friends and lovers, as well as nations and religions. When an individual, group or nation is treated with respect, on the other hand, they sense it and it affects their sense of themselves and how they respond to you.

Self-centred absorption is also a part of the road to paranoia. When you become completely absorbed with yourself, the whole world revolves only around you and you feel grandiose, tremendously important. In this frame of mind, everything is taken personally, in a self-referential manner. If someone is not giving you the honour and attention you deserve, that person is cast out of your life.

When you are absorbed with yourself, you want the good only for yourself, not others. You are driven to protect yourself and all that you identify with. At the same time, you reject others. Once again, this is a continuum. It's normal for all of us to have moments like these, but unchecked the self-centred mind can grow and become your basic way of being in the world.

Self-centred absorption does not express the basic truth of who you are, living a self-centred life; you are simply encasing yourself in a cocoon that creates more of a prison than a safe resting place. In order to dissolve paranoia, you must learn how to unravel the cocoon created by the self-centred mind. At first this can be frightening, because the cocoon feels so familiar and safe. However, the longer you stay inside it, the more insulated you are from the world and the less you understand and know how to respond to it. This cocoon itself puts you in danger. The safest place is out in the air, under the broad open sky, where risks abound.

Risks abound?

Yes! There are no guarantees when you approach someone with a challenging conversation that all difficulties will be resolved, particularly if you know the other person is adopting a malevolent mind.

> *And the trouble is, if you don't risk anything, you risk even more.*
>
> – Erica Jong[102]

The biggest risk is not taking any risk.

— Mark Zuckerberg[103]

To save all we must risk all.

— Friedrich von Schiller[104]

So, if this risky business of dealing with challenging conversations is that important, let's move to the next practical stage of how we ensure that we see fear as the trickster and bully it is, and choose thinking that is exclusive of fear to deal successfully with challenging conversations.

Adopt the love paradigm as a mindset.

> *Do you want me to tell you something really very subversive? Love is everything it's cracked up to be. That's why people are so cynical about it. It really is worth fighting for, being brave for, risking everything for. And the trouble is, if you don't risk anything, you risk even more.*
>
> — Erica Jong, *Fear of Flying*[105]

So, let's go to the next section and learn how!

Adopting the love mindset

If you want to find peace, do peace.

— Rabbi Eleazar ben Azariah[106]

Resist not evil.

— Jesus's words, Matthew 5:39

At first glance, "resist not evil" seems to be confusing and illogical. It appears not only contradictory to the previous chapter's arguments, but contrary to the holy scriptures. However, as we look more closely at the application of dealing with challenging conversations, we see this truth to be simple, logical, and life changing.

As Deepak Chopra points out,[107] people seem to assume that the very moment you brand someone as evil (terrorists, Nazis, mass murderers, pedophiles, etc.), you have every right to seek revenge against them. The war on terror is based on this notion. The first person to disagree however, happened to be Jesus. If you look at the passage in the New Testament where Jesus says to turn the other cheek (Matthew 5:38–42), the whole speech illustrates how radical Jesus's morality actually was.

He says, in modern words:

> You've been taught an eye for an eye and a tooth for a tooth, but I say don't resist evil.
>
> If someone hits you, let him hit you twice.
>
> If someone sues you in court to get your coat, give it to him and your cloak too.
>
> If someone forces you to go one mile, go two.
>
> If someone asks you for something, give it to him. If he wants to borrow money, don't turn your back.

Now, it's clear that no one, Christian or otherwise, lives up to these injunctions.

Christ's words were radical and revolutionary. His instruction on how to love more completely is opposite to what most think and do, yet these truths are the very keys to unlocking a life of goodness in the midst of an evil world, where operating from a paradigm of fear is predominant.

God is love. Jesus taught his disciples how to choose a paradigm of love and therefore resist evil. To live love is a higher level of living. To approach a challenging conversation from a mental set of love is to move radically to a higher level of communication, leadership and interpersonal problem solving.

To avoid any oversimplification and misconception of the practicality and simplicity of choosing, one second at a time, the paradigm of love, let me point out that when we are assaulted physically our natural response is to protect ourselves, often done by striking back. Man's autonomic nervous system produces involuntary responses. This means when we are confronted with danger, we respond involuntarily. The heart automatically starts beating faster, pupils dilate, perspiration begins, and we immediately make ready to protect ourselves. If an arrow were shot at your head, without thought you would automatically move out of the way. These involuntary responses are a part of the nervous system connected on both sides of the spinal column. They are not involuntary responses because they are not a conscious function of the mind.

The trickster fear, however, understands how our bodies work and tries to use this against us to involve us in fear-based evil. When someone verbally attacks us with hate, anger, or disrespect, our autonomic nervous system may very well go into operation. With the momentum moving in the direction of defending and attacking back, we are tempted to respond to evil with evil. We cannot control the involuntary responses, but the mind's resistance to evil can and should be controlled. We are not to resist evil. If we respond to evil with evil, we will be drawn in and become part of what we resist.

*Ye have heard that it hath been said, an eye for an
eye, and a tooth for a tooth: But I say unto you, that
ye resist not evil: but who so ever shall smite thee on
thy right cheek, turn to him the other also.*

– Matthew 5:38,39

"Smite thee on thy right cheek" is not referring to being
punched or smacked hard. God never wants his people to endure
physical abuse. If this happens, you have no choice but to protect
yourself. Many scriptures teach we are to defend ourselves if
someone is trying physically to hurt us. The above expression was
understood in the Oriental culture as a very great insult. In their
culture, to touch the cheek of another man was a humiliating
insult. The essence of what is being said here is, if someone insults
you, do not respond in kind. Let him do it again.

The normal course of action is this: if someone insults us, we
insult him. If someone curses at us, we curse at him. If someone
yells at us, we yell at him. When this is our response, we have been
baited, hooked, and pulled into the dark side of fear. Now we are
participating in evil because we resisted it.

How very clever and calculated this whirlpool of evil is.
When evil attacks we already have the momentum of involuntary
responses working, and we also have to contend with our pride.
"Who does that guy think he is, talking to me like that?" "Nobody
insults me and gets away with it." "Where I come from, we don't
put up with that kind of behaviour." "You talking to *me*?" Pride is
a driving emotion that will take us for a negative ride. Pride comes
before a fall. Fear-based thought choice comes before a fall in the
middle of a challenging conversation.

We have one life to live. Each day has only twenty-four
hours. How much of our lives do we want to spend in defiance
of man's ordinances? One minute wasted on such matters of little

importance is one minute lost in our very short lives. Do you want to fight city hall or live love's way?

> *Therefore if thine enemy hunger, feed him; if he thirst, give him a drink: for in so doing thou shalt heap coals of fire on his head.*

— Romans 12:20

"Heap coals of fire on his head" is an Eastern idiom. In the small Eastern villages, one person would rise first and start the fire for the village. A boy would then take the burning coals in a piece of pottery, balance it on top of his head, and deliver it to the other households. This was a pleasant task for the boy, because in the cold of the morning the coals warmed him. With our love we can warm our enemies. Our good can overcome our evil.

The best summary statement concerning the practice of love is: overcome evil with good.

Does this mean we let people run all over us? Do we let people push us around with evil words? No! What it means in practice is taking a bold, courageous stand. Living love is not being passive, letting others run over you. Love is assertive, even aggressive. Love is attacking in the name of love, not in the name of fear. Fear's aim is destruction. Love's aim is deliverance. Thank goodness they are mutually exclusive!

Contrary to popular belief, hatred is not at all difficult to release. When you are in a dark room, all that is needed is a little bit of light to make the darkness disappear. The same is true with hatred: all that is needed is compassion when entering the situation, and the darkness of hatred quickly subsides.

It's easy to get rid of an enemy. Take them to lunch. Let them be the star. Think of ways you can give to them. Turn them into a friend.

There are different ways of releasing hatred and developing forgiveness, but the first requirement is the willingness to do so.

At the beginning of my workshops as a presenter/consultant, I invariably invite the participants to study the following:

COMMITMENT

Until one is committed, there is hesitancy, the chance to draw back, always ineffectiveness.

Concerning all acts of initiative (and creation) there is one elementary truth, the ignorance of which kills countless ideas and splendid plans: that the moment one definitely commits oneself, then Providence moves too.

All sorts of things occur to help one that otherwise never would have occurred. A whole stream of events issue from the decision, raising in one's favour all manner of unforeseen incidents and meetings of material assistance, which no man could have dreamt would have come his way. I have learned deep respect for one of Goethe's couplets:

"Whatever you can do or dream you can, begin it. Boldness has genius, power, and magic in it."

– W.N. Murray, *The Scottish Himalayan Expedition*, 1951[108]

I then suggest that if they are not committed to the objective of the workshop, they should leave. So spend your time being truthful to where your real intentions take you.

Similarly, there's more than one proven way of dealing successfully with challenging conversations, even hatred and violence, but the first requirement is to commit to doing so, solely from a thought-choice mental set of love, not fear.

As the Chinese proverb states: "Every journey of a thousand miles begins with the first step."

The first step in the practice of love is the commitment to the intent and willingness to do so.

If you don't really want to release your hatred, if you think you need to hold on to it because it serves and protects you, it will be an impediment.

Each interaction you have with another person presents the possibility of Heaven or Hell. It's good to be able to choose your own destination and not be ruled by anger and fear that automatically arises and tries to run the show.

Forgiveness—the highest form of love—does not mean remaining in a toxic or abusive relationship or participating in something that is harmful for you. It simply means letting go of the anger you feel and wishing the best for the other person. When you do so, you become able to make healthy choices for yourself.

You can't control the way another behaves, but you can control how you choose to respond. Choose love, choose health. Don't choose to be caught in the quagmire of pain. When you are determined to see others only as good or bad, you limit your perception of them and aren't able see them, or yourself, in the largest context possible. Furthermore, whichever you choose, you will reap what you sow.

Life is a process in constant flux, in which we all contain everything. Whatever another human being has experienced is also within you. As the flow of life is constant, someone who is very angry one moment always has the possibility of waking up and being filled with love the next. There is always the possibility of change, growth, and renewal for everyone. When you see others in that light you help them grow, and you are living a life of forgiveness. You are also removing yourself from the trap of the malevolent mind that keeps you chained to fear.

When you live a life based on forgiveness, you cannot be harmed. And the power that comes to you to be constructive and joyous is enormous.

Don Henley's song "The Heart of the Matter," which stresses the importance of forgiveness, is said by the artist to have taken "forty-eight years to write and three minutes to sing."

What you do by making appropriately positive thought choices is build a mental set of faith. Faith keeps us standing tall no matter what happens. In each of us there is a candle, but in some it is not yet lit. Our job is to keep this candle burning.

Hmmm . . . interesting realization: In the moment of commitment, has providence moved? Henley's song referred to above is recorded on the Eagles' album "Hell Freezes Over," surely a powerful image of what we can expect when we practice, internalize, and habituate these deeds of love! Also, a whole stream of events issues from the decision. The eagle is the only bird, ornithologists tell us, that chooses in times of storm to get out of the bushes and rocks where all the other birds hide, and face the storm in order to rise above it. Surely that's what leaders are called to do when facing the storms of challenging conversations.

How do we freeze hell over?

Find something that is good and beautiful and do it every day. When you are busy doing that, fear will no longer have a hold on you.

Deep within each of us there is a strong sense of what is meaningful, what we value and respect. Some are in touch with this, others not. However, whether you realize it or not, your inner self reacts negatively whenever you go against your true values and that which has real meaning for you. The price you pay for this is a lack of self-respect.

On the road to becoming fearless, it is essential to get in touch with your innate sense of what you truly value. When you sell out, when you violate your inner trust, you become easy prey for self-hatred. An excellent antidote to this is living a life you can respect.

When you truly respect yourself you cannot disrespect another. You automatically see what is valuable in others and respond in a positive manner. As you do so, you begin to live a life worthy of respect.

We've all made mistakes, some more serious than others. But everything can be repaired when we're not mired in self-hatred. Self-hatred keeps all wounds alive and makes us feel guilty much of the time. Many people think that by feeling guilty they're doing something worthwhile, repairing what they've done wrong. But in fact they're not. Guilt, a substitute for true reparations, is toxic in many ways, and often prevents you from taking action which would make the necessary corrections and move forward.

See what is needed and do it today. The actions you take will be deeds of love and respect—for yourself, and for the world you live in. These deeds turn mistakes into growth and benefit everyone. Because it is impossible not to make mistakes, the real question is, Have you done what is needed to repair them? Have you turned your errors into beneficial actions or a foundation for a life worth living?

Deeds of love heal wounds and prevent fear from rising. Love is not necessarily a feeling. Love is a verb, an action you can take no matter how you are feeling. You can always offer deeds of love. There are many actions to take which become blessings to you and the entire world.

When you offer deeds of love, you are receiving protection against the effects of anger. When thoughts of anger or hatred arise, immediately replace them with a deed of love. As you bless others in this way, you are blessed as well. And as you do this, you will see your life expand and prosper. No deed of love offered goes unappreciated, no matter who you offer it to.

Happiness comes from being loving, not from being loved.

— Erich Fromm[109]

It's easy to find out what your deeds of love are. For each person it's different. Take some time and make a list of deeds that are meaningful to you. What makes you feel loved? Which deeds express your love for others? Some people need to receive gifts, cards, and flowers, while others feel cared for when a friend promptly returns a phone call or shows up on time. For others, it is very important that their friends keep their word. Any breach of trust makes them feel unloved.

Think of some actions you take that express your concern and love. Again, this differs from person to person. Some examples might be cooking a meal for another person, visiting a friend in the hospital, or running errands for a neighbour who needs the help. Take the time to find out how you enjoy giving to others and what others actually need. It's important to ask others how you can be of service and find out what matters to them.

Compare the deeds of love on your list with the deeds you do each day. There may be a discrepancy. Take some of the deeds of love on your list and include them in your daily living. No matter what mood you're in, do at least one a day. It's especially good to do these deeds for those you're having difficulty with. By thinking of them kindly, by extending yourself, not only will you wipe out your own negativity, but you will learn to see them in a totally new way.

As we bless others, so are we blessed.

We have the power to offer blessings, which encourage, enhance, and uplift all of life. The words you speak to others can be powerful forces for good. When you do not take charge of your words, when you speak negatively toward someone rather than lifting them up, you are tearing them down. Our intentions have a strong impact on our relationships and the outcome of our activities. By offering a blessing, you are sending a deep intention and wish for a person, activity, or project to flourish.

Whenever you become aware of having a negative thought about someone, stop and bless them instead. Say, "I send you a blessing for all the goodness you desire come into your life. I bless you for health and well-being."

You can bless and enhance activities and projects as well. When you offer a blessing to the work you do, or to a project you or someone else is involved in, you are taking time to send powerful, loving energy to it. As you regularly practice offering blessings to others and to yourself, you will be amazed at how your health, well-being, and joy in life will be enhanced. Difficult, challenging conversations will simply become conversations.

Summary

- Practice love habits. Replace fear-based habits.
- Perfect love casts out fear.
- Forgiveness is the highest form of love.

Let's get to the heart of the matter:
In order to get me through the night (of fear)
Study, absorb, inwardly digest
Develop, master, and choose habits of a love mindset.

Points to Ponder

Paraphrasing the work of Brenda Shoshanna:

Forgiveness starts with a willingness to forgive both others and yourself.

Forgiveness is a process that needs to be done regularly, like brushing your teeth and taking a shower. Just saying "I forgive you" is one step. It may not be enough. To root out the depth of your anger or resentment, the forgiveness workout is wonderful. As you do the steps regularly, it becomes impossible to stay angry. After doing it one day, a certain amount of anger may be released. If more arises, it doesn't mean you haven't succeeded, it just means there's another layer there still. Keep doing the workout until you feel totally clear and loving.

1. Turn hatred into goodwill

Think for a moment of people you do not like or respect. What thoughts do you think about them? How do they respond? Now become aware of the negative thoughts you think about yourself. What is this doing to you?

Focus on the effect your lack of forgiveness is having on you. How often do you think of the person? How much energy are you giving? How is your lack of forgiveness blocking you in other ways?

Ask yourself if you're willing to release your hatred, to get it out of your life. If you are not, stop for a moment and become aware of the toll it takes on you. Has it hurt the person you are angry at as much as it has hurt you?

In order to be able to be free of anger, do not justify the hatred in any way. See it as a poison. When it arises, simply experience the feeling for what it is: an unpleasant emotion. Do not repress or deny the energy, just experience it fully and then let it go. Say goodbye to it, see it drifting away. The ability to stay steady and centred during the experience of hatred without lashing out is a mark of a mature person.

Another way to dissolve hatred is to remind yourself that what you give the other person you simultaneously receive in return. If you give anger, you will receive anger. If you offer compassion and forgiveness, you will receive it simultaneously.

Forget the story that keeps anger alive. Much of your anger and hatred is kept going by the story you tell yourself and others about it. Do not focus on the story you are telling yourself or the reasons to keep the hatred going. This story is just something you've made up. If you make up another story, if you dream up different interpretations for what happened, the hatred won't be there. In fact, you might even experience compassion or love.

Find ways in which you are similar. When someone you are suspicious or afraid of comes into your life, stop immediately. Find something you like about the person, ways in which you are similar, ways in which you could lend a helping hand. Break into your projections. Ask questions. Listen to what they tell you. Find out who the person truly is, what's important to them.

Remember all the person has done for you. When you're in the grip of hatred, it's easy to forget the larger picture in the relationship, all that has gone on. Now consciously bring to mind all the ways that person has benefited you. Remember his kindnesses to you. Think of qualities he has that you respect.

Also remember times you may have behaved the same way he did. Can you now forgive yourself, as well as forgiving him? If you think the person deserves hatred, stop for a moment and become aware that he may be confused about how to find happiness, and that his negative behaviour is a reflection of him, not you. It is not personal, but an expression of his own unhappiness. No one who knows himself and is fulfilled is harmful to others. See the person as someone in pain lashing out, calling for help. It's important to know that obnoxiousness is a cry for help.

How about you?

Make a list of what he's done that you disrespect. Now once again compare this with your own life. See if you indulge in these actions as well. If so, determine right now to eliminate them. Take a deep breath. Don't create guilt or make all this into a pressure.

Take it as a fascinating adventure. Realize that this is a potent exercise in releasing fear, self-hatred, hatred of others, and learning to live a life based on self-respect.

Forgive yourself. If you cannot forgive yourself for something, ask yourself what you need to do to wipe the slate clean, forgive yourself, and start again. If you truly ask, eventually you will realize what is needed for reconciliation. Then do it. If you cannot do it with the person you have offended, do it with someone else. You do not need the forgiveness of another person to forgive yourself, you simply need to know what you need to feel all right about the situation now. Once you can forgive yourself, it is so much easier to forgive others as well.

Forgiveness and extending love are two sides of the same coin.

The ancient exercise below is another means of offering forgiveness to others and yourself.

2. Consciously extend love

There is a beautiful meditation practice in Tibetan Buddhism called *Tonglen*. One part of it is this: Whenever you are upset with anyone (including yourself), simply send love. Even if you don't feel love, say, "I send love and light to you." It is the intention that matters, not what you happen to feel. Just keep sending love and light, no matter how you feel. Send this to yourself as well, and to any negative situation you are confronted with.

This is an amazing practice. It produces a real effect. The people to whom you're sending love and light feel it on some level. They often begin to respond differently. You also feel it. Just doing this in a focused and intentional way dissolves your own hatred and hurt.

This is such a simple exercise and yet so powerful. Some people resist doing it. They are holding on to their upset and hate. If that happens to you, simply send love and light to your resistance, and send love and light to your hatred. If you prefer your hatred, you can always stop. But why not relent for a little while and give this a try? Just do it. If you still resist this exercise, listen to the Eagles' song "Get Over It"!

3. Forgiveness doesn't change the person who hurt you; forgiveness changes you

This closing point to ponder was eloquently expressed by Crystal Smith [116] when he pointed out that forgiveness does not mean you forget. It's a ridiculous idea to believe that you forgive and forget. You don't forget; but you do have the opportunity to forgive every time you remember those who have impacted you in a negative way. If I don't forgive other[s], I hold myself hostage to a prison that God never intended for me to stay within.

Forgiveness is not a one-time, fix-all ... it's a daily sacrifice that I have to implement so that I can receive what it is that God has for me!

BIBLIOGRAPHY

[1]   1. Shackel, D. (2012). *Five Seconds at a Time: How Leaders Make the Impossible Possible*. Toronto: Harper Collins.

[2]   John 15:13

[3]   17. Shackel, D. (2012). *Five Seconds at a Time: How Leaders Make the Impossible Possible*. Toronto: Harper Collins, Pg. 19.

[4]   Carey, J. Commencement address at the 2014 Maharashi University graduation. https://www.youtube.com/watch?v=V80-gPkpH6M

[5]   Holiday, R. (2017). *Ego is the Enemy*. New York: Penguin.

[6]   James, W. (1902). *The Varieties of Religious Experience*. New York: Longmans (there are now 273 editions).

[7]   Assaraf, J. (2018). *Innercize: The new science to Unlock Your Brain's hidden Power*. Cardiff: Waterside Press.

[8]   Aitchison, S., (2011) *100 Ways to develop Your Mind*. Scotland: CYTGuides.com

[9]   Proverbs 29:18

[10]   Roosevelt, T. (2015). *Theodore Roosevelt on Bravery: Lessons from the Most Courageous Leader of the Twentieth Century*. Skyhorse Publishing, Inc., p. 5.

[11]   Murray W.H. (1951). *The Scottish Himalayan Expedition*. London: J. M. Dent and Sons

[12]   Stone, D., Patton, B., Heen, S. (1999). *Difficult Conversations: How to Discuss What Matters Most*. New York: Random House.

[13]   Ibid.

[14]   Diamond, J., 1997. *Guns, Germs, and Steel*. New York: W. W. Norton & Co.

[15]   — — — (1997). *Guns, Germs, and Steel*. New York: W. W. Norton & Co., p.154

[16]   Gibbon, E. (1776). *The Decline and Fall of the Roman Empire*. New York: Modern Library; Reprint edition (March 1, 2005).

17   — — — (1776). *The Decline and Fall of the Roman Empire.* New York: Modern Library; Reprint edition (March 1, 2005), p.32

18   Patterson, K. Grenny, J. McMillan, R., and Switzler, A. (2002). *Crucial Conversations: Tools for Talking When Stakes Are High.* New York: McGraw Hill.

19   Stone, D., Patton, B., Heen, S. (1999). *Difficult Conversations: How to Discuss What Matters Most.* New York: Random House.

20   Patterson, K. Grenny, J. McMillan, R., Switzler, A. (2002). *Crucial Conversations: Tools for Talking When Stakes Are High.* New York: McGraw Hill, pg. 9.

21   McCall, M.W., Lombardo, M.M., Morrison, A.M. (2010). *The Lessons of Experience: How Successful Executives Develop on the Job.* Lexington: Lexington Press.

22   Worthington, E. (1999). *Hope-Focused Marriage Counseling.* Downers Grove, IL: IVP Academic, pg. 42.

23   Sinha, M. (2012). "Family Violence in Canada: A Statistical Profile". Juristat Article, Statistics Canada, No 85-002X.

24   National Crime Victimization (2011). Bureau of Justice Statistics, US Department of Justice.

25   Stone, D., Patton, B., Heen, S. (1999). *Difficult Conversations: How to Discuss What Matters Most.* New York: Random House.

26   Patterson, K. Grenny, J. McMillan, R., Switzler, A. (2002). *Crucial Conversations: Tools for Talking When Stakes Are High.* New York: McGraw Hill.

27   Ibid.

28   Stone, D., Patton, B., Heen, S. (1999). *Difficult Conversations: How to Discuss What Matters Most.* New York: Random House.

29   Patterson, K. Grenny, J. McMillan, R., and Switzler, A. (2002). *Crucial Conversations: Tools for Talking When Stakes Are High.* New York: McGraw Hill.

30   — — — (2005). *Crucial Confrontations: Tools for Resolving Broken Promises, Violated Expectations and Bad Behaviour.* New York: McGraw Hill.

31   Gallagher, R. (2009). *How to Tell Anyone Anything: Handling Difficult Conversations at Work.* New York: Amazon.

32   Toynbee, A. J. (1948). *Civilization on Trial.* New York: Oxford University Press.

33   Gallagher, R. (2009). *How to Tell Anyone Anything: Handling Difficult Conversations at Work.* New York: Amazon.

34   Patterson, K. Grenny, J. McMillan, R., Switzler, A. (2002). *Crucial Conversations: Tools for Talking When Stakes Are High.* New York: McGraw Hill.

35   Shwom, B., Snyder, L.G., Clarke, L. (2016). *Business Communication.* Toronto: Pearson.

36   Butler, S. (1663). *Hudibras.* Assorted.

37   Beckham, A. (2013). https://www.youtube.com/watch?v=kSR4xuU07sc Boulder, CO: TEDx Talks.

38   Kouzes, J.M. Posner, B.Z. (1997). *The Leadership Challenge.* San Francisco: Jossey-Bass.

39   Solum, M. New Leader Records 1924-2008. Business Files Series iv, Archival Collections, Columbia University Libraries.

40   — — — New Leader Records 1924-2008. Business Files Series iv, Archival Collections, Columbia University Libraries, p. 48

41   Ginott, H. G., (1972) *Teacher and Child: A Book for Teachers and Parents,* New York: Random House.

42   Allen, J. M. (1902). *As a Man Thinketh.* London: Oxford Press.

43   Ibid.

44   Senge, P. (1990). *The Fifth Discipline.* New York; Doubleday.

45   Seigel, D. (2012). *Mindsight: The New Science of Personal Transformation.* New York: Penguin.

46   Doige, N. (2016). *The Brain That Changes Itself.* New York: Penguin.

47   Taylor, J.B. (2014). *My Stroke of Insight.* New York: Wiley.

48   Pillay, S. (2011). *Your Brain and Business: The Neuroscience of Great Leaders.* New Jersey: FT Press

49   Perls, F. (1998). *Gestalt Therapy.* New York: Simon & Schuster, pg. 28.

50   Neibuhr, R., quoted in Wilson, K.G., and DuFrene, T. (2012) *The Wisdom to Know the Difference.* Oakland: Harbinger Press.

51   Liberman, V. et al. (2009). "Happiness and memory". *Emotion,* p. 666

52   Shoshanna, B. (2010). *Fearless: The 7 Principles of Peace of Mind.* New York: Sterling Ethos

53   Franklin D. Roosevelt, Inaugural Address, March 4, 1993. (1938) In Rosenman, S (ed.) *The Public Papers of Franklin D. Roosevelt, Volume 2: The Year of Crisis.* New York: Rambling House, p. 11–12

54   Giacalone, R. A., Paul, K., and Jurkiewicz, C.L. (2005). "A Preliminary Investigation into the Role of Positive Psychology in Consumer Sensitivity to Corporate Social Performance". *Journal of Business Ethics,* 58(4): p.295–305.

55   Clarke, N. (2010). "Emotional Intelligence and its Relationship to Transformational Leadership and Key Project Manager Competencies". *Project Management Journal*, 41(2), p.5–20.

56   Pillay, S. (2011). *Your Brain and Business: The Neuroscience of Great Leaders*. New Jersey: FT Press

57   Walton, T.B. (1983). *Psychology Stand Behavior*. London: Longwood press.

58   Clarke N. (2010). "The Impact of a Training Programme Designed to Target the Emotional Intelligence abilities of Project Managers". *International Journal of Project Management*. 28(5): p.461–468.

59   Morton, D.L. et al. (2009). "Reproductivity of Placebo Analgesia: Effects of Dispositional Optimism." *Pain*.

60   Covey, S. (1989). *Seven Habits of Highly Effective People*. New York: Simon and Schuster.

61   Olson, J. (2013). *The Slight Edge*. Austin: The Greenleaf Press.

62   Feldman, M. L. and Spratt, M.F. (1998). "Five Frogs on a Log: A CEO's Field Guide to Accelerating the Transition in Mergers, Acquisitions and Gut-Wrenching Change". *Engineering*, December.

63   Emerson, R.W, (1841). *Essays: First Series*. Hurst & Company: New York

64   Watson, T. (1956). "Formula For Success". Quotes.net

65   Watson, T.J. www.brainyquote.com

66   Clarke, J., Quote from DVD "Your Summit Awaits". www.Starthrower.com

67   Bonhoeffer, D. (2006). *Wonderously Sheltered*. Amazon.com

68   Sinek, S. (2019). *The Infinite Game*. New York: Portfolio Penguin.

69   Walsh, N.D. (2017). *Conversations with God*. Virginia: Rainbow Ridge Books.

70   Keen S. (2013). *Fire in the belly: On Being a man*. New York: Thriftbooks

71   Remen, R.N. (2006). Kitchen Table Wisdom. New York: Penguin Group.

72   Mehrabian, A. (1972), *Nonverbal Communication*. New York: Routledge.

73   — — —, (1970). *Tactics of Social Influence*, London: Prentice Hall

74   Fromm, E. (1976). To *Have or to Be: The Nature of the Psyche*. AbeBooks.com

75   Lathrap, M.T. (2016), *The Poems and Written Addresses of Mary T. Lathrap*. New York: Palapa Press

76 Minchin, T. (2010). "Nine Life Lessons". Address given to graduates of University of Western Australia. YouTube.

77 Robinson, M. (2008) *What are we Doing Here?: Essays*. New York: McClelland and Stewart.

78 Winfrey, O. (2018). *The Path Made Clear*. New York: Flatiron Press.

79 Jung, C. (2009). *The Red Book*. New York: W. W. Norton.

80 Dyer, W. (2014*). I Can See Clearly Now*. New York: Hay House.

81 Maslow, A. (1998). *Towards a Psychology of Being*. New York: Van Nostrand.

82 Rumi, J.A. (1997). *The Illuminated Rumi*. New York: Harmony Books.

83 Buber, M. (1937). *I and Thou*. New York: Charles Scribner Press.

84 Buddha, G., (Carus Paul Ed.) (1957). Books.Google.com

85 Wheeler, M. (2015) *Negotiation*. New York: Penguin.

86 Ziglar, Z. (2017). *Born to Win*. Washington: Made for Success Publishing.

87 Williamson, M., (1996) *A Return to Love*. New York: Harper One.

88 Tillich, P. (1997). *The Courage to Be*. New York: Yale University Press.

89 "Robin Williams Death: Police Confirm Suicide". www.bbc.com, Nov. 7, 2014.

90 Thoreau, H.D. (2006). *Nature and Other Essays*. New York: Dover Publications

91 Emerson, R.W. (2015). Top 10 Ralph Waldo Emerson Quotes. BrainyQuotes.com

92 Duhigg, C. (2014). *The Power of Habit*. New York: Random House.

93 Peck M.S. (2003). *The Road Less Traveled*. New York: Simon and Schuster.

94 Ghandi, M. "Snake Bite Poisoning". Cited by Bawaska H.S. and Bawaska, P.H. *Journal of Mahatma Ghandi Institute of Medical Science*, 2015. 20:5–14.

95 Lorrance, A. (1978). *The Love Project*. L. P. Publications

96 Lao Tzu (Translator, B.B .Walker) (1997). *The Tao Ching of Lao Tzu*. New York: Essential Wisdom Library.

97 Homes W. "Buddhism Under the Communists". *China Quarterly*, No. 6 April-June, 1966.

98 Bennett, R.T. (2016). *The Light in the Heart*. Self-published.

99 Barker, J. A. (1993). *Paradigms: Business of Discovering the Future*. New York: Harper Business.

100 Dunnigan, N. (2014). *Zen Stories of the Samurai*. Morrisville, N.C.: Lulu Publications.

101 Heller, J. (1984). *Catch 22*. New York: Simon and Schuster.

102 Jong, E. (2001). *Fear of Fifty*. New York: Penguin Group.

103 Kelly, H. "Facebook CEO Mark Zuckerberg's Power Move May be the Biggest Game-Changer for the Job Market". *Forbes*, May 22, 2020.

104 Thomas, C. (1954). *The life and Work of Fredrich Schiller*. Oxford: Claredon Press.

105 Jong, E. (1973). *Fear of Flying*. New York: Penguin Group.

106 Mindel, N. (1953). *Rabbi Elazar ben Azariah*. New York: Kehot Publication Society.

107 Nicholas, M.P. (2010). *The Lost Art of Listening*. New York: Guilford Press.

108 Murray, W. H. (1951). *The Scottish Himalayan Expedition*. Darlington: J. M. Dent & Co.

109 Fromm, E. (1976). *To Have or to Be: The Nature of the Psyche*. AbeBooks. com

110 Brainyquote.com, 2020

111 Baudelaire, C., "Charles Baudelaire Poems" literatureessaysamples. com. 2016.

112 Churchill, Winston https//www.brainyquote.com

113 Sinek, S. (2009) *Start With Why*. New York: Portfolio Penguin

114 Spectator (world's oldest magazine). March 2018

115 Peterson, Jordan B. (2018) *12 Rules of Life: An Antidote to Chaos*. Toronto:Penguin Random House

116 Smith, Crystal, *Facebook Reel*, August 21, 2023

117 Tolle, Eckhart, *The Power of Now: A Guide to Spiritual Enlightenment*. California:Namaste Publishing, 2004

118 Kant, I. [1805], Critique of Judgment. Translated by J.H. Bernard. New York:Dover Publications, 2004

POSTSCRIPT #1

"I think I wear my hypocrisy on my sleeve. I would never say I'm not a complete hypocrite."

Bo Burnham [110]

The text is virtually complete, the publishers are drafting the book cover, and the manuscript is about to be sent to the printing press. But how can I publish this work without also acknowledging the relative ease to put in writing practical suggestions on how best to deal with challenging conversations, yet not implement practices myself!

Over the last few years of my married life, I have written this book and yet failed fully to honour my promise to my wife that I would be true only to her. Involving myself with a female colleague, now strikes me as a betrayal and breaking of my marriage vows. I knew in my heart of hearts that I was sinning, but fear of being rejected and the collapse of my 24 years of marriage made it easier to cater to my ego and false self. I kept sending, and receiving personal emails without sharing them with my wife! Being caught catapulted me into a turbulent period of marriage discord with likelihood of separation. In hindsight I realized that while loving my wife, I had lacked the courage to confront her with feelings of not receiving the ego-stroking I thought I needed and gained from my friend.

Why make this public confession and admission? It is hoped that the reader sees my hypocrisy as evidence of my remorsefulness and my illustrating in my personal life just how challenging difficult conversations are, even when you know what should be done and can preach a good line. The French poet Charles Baudelaire [111] began an essay with the words, "Hypocrite reader my fellow, my brother" in an attempt to suggest the universality of not always practicing what we preach. It is my personal hope that my disclosure does nothing but strengthen the seriousness of the need to develop the courage to care enough to confront and thus avoid the sort of agony I have had to endure before being forgiven by the grace of God ... as well as my wife.

Perhaps the main justification to include this Postscript is to disclose the truth that after I had realized the folly of my betrayal, did I practice what I had written about. The chapter on fear, the chapter on listening and Pillay's five steps presented as CIRCA in chapter 4 became my step-by-step process to communicate more effectively with my wife. I am certain that our marriage will now last unto death do us part, but that the material presented within this text has enabled us both to rekindle our loving relationship and reap the joys therein. My personal life has become a testimony to the practical validity, power and efficacy of the "ABCs of Challenging Conversations".

To close and In summary, "a leader is a custodian of the human spirit and challenging conversations are successfully dealt with only when we adopt the higher ground of love". [p.56].

POSTSCRIPT #2

Closing Propitious Points to Ponder

Q1: Why a Postscript #2?

A1: This whole text has been written as a sequel to my first book *Five Seconds at a Time.*

The Postscript presented there was meant primarily as a tribute to my sister Kathleen who, within one year of tragically losing her beloved husband Bruce, demonstrated inspirational courage to "stand up straight with shoulders back" and face Mount Ruapehu which represented a horrific reminder of Bruce's demise, as well as a painful representation of death, loss, ultimate sacrifice and [even worse] betrayal.

What did she do? Yes... you guessed it ... ***she climbed the wretched mountain!***

Talk about **courage,** which Winston Churchill [112] reminded us is the highest of human qualities. What an "eagle", which ornithologists report is the only bird who in times of storm, <u>chooses</u> to leave the nest, face and fly ***into*** the storm ... in order to use the power of the storm to rise up above it!

Q2: What's the point besides demonstrating heroic courage?

A2: She told me *after* conquering her fear and anxiety by actually accomplishing standing at the peak of the mountain, that her "why" as Simon Sinek [113] would word it, was to carry a large pack containing canned foods, water bottles, blankets and medical supplies in order to **stock the hut** ... on the off-chance that someone else may find themselves in the predicament that her younger brother found himself during the longest night of his life.

Q3: Why repeat this super compassionate act of heroic proportions?

A3: I chose to close this book with equivalent recognition, admiration and love for my fellow Professor Emeritus of psychology from the University of Toronto, Dr. Jordan Peterson, photographed here with my beloved wife Mary Lynn.

Peterson's books, podcasts, and most importantly his character have been a source of encouragement paralleled by my sister Kathleen.

Little wonder the Spectator describes Jordan as "one of the most important thinkers to emerge on the world stage for many years" [114].

Thank you, Jordan!

BTW if you don't yet know Jordan's work start with his "12 Rules of Life" [115] where he presents as Rule 1 the need for us all to follow Kathleen's example and "stand up straight with shoulders back", pick up your cross and keep climbing!